Elite • 178

Hatamoto
Samurai Horse and Foot Guards 1540–1724

STEPHEN TURNBULL ILLUSTRATED BY RICHARD HOOK
Consultant editor Martin Windrow

First published in Great Britain in 2010 by Osprey Publishing,
Midland House, West Way, Botley, Oxford OX2 0PH, UK
44-02 23rd St, Suite 219, Long Island City, NY 11101
Email: info@ospreypublishing.com

© 2010 Osprey Publishing Ltd.

All rights reserved. Apart from any fair dealing for the purpose of private study, research, criticism or review, as permitted under the Copyright, Designs and Patents Act, 1988, no part of this publication may be reproduced, stored in a retrieval system, or transmitted in any form or by any means, electronic, electrical, chemical, mechanical, optical, photocopying, recording or otherwise, without the prior written permission of the copyright owner. Enquiries should be addressed to the Publishers.

Print ISBN: 978 184603 478 7
ebook ISBN: 978 184908 251 8

Editor: Martin Windrow
Design: Ken Vail Graphic Design, Cambridge, UK (kvgd.com)
Typeset in Sabon and Myriad Pro
Index by Fineline Editorial Services
Originated by PDQ Digital Media Solutions
Printed in China through World Print Ltd.

10 11 12 13 14   10 9 8 7 6 5 4 3 2 1

A CIP catalogue record for this book is available from the British Library

FOR A CATALOGUE OF ALL BOOKS PUBLISHED BY OSPREY MILITARY AND AVIATION PLEASE CONTACT:

North America:
Osprey Direct, c/o Random House Distribution Center,
400 Hahn Road, Westminster, MD 21157
E-mail: info@ospreydirectusa.com

All other regions:
Osprey Direct UK, PO Box 140, Wellingborough,
Northants NN8 2FA, UK
E-mail: info@ospreydirect.co.uk

www.ospreypublishing.com

GLOSSARY

ashigaru	footsoldier(s)
bakufu	the shogunate, lit. 'government within the curtain'
daimyo	feudal lord
fudai	'inner' lords, hereditary retainers
gundan	war band – the vassals from whom a daimyo's army was formed
gokenin	houseman, low-ranking retainer
han	a daimyo's fief
hata	flag
hatamoto	a daimyo's staff and household troops – those 'beneath the flag'
jinaichō	a temple town
kagemusha	retainer who impersonates the daimyo to protect him
karō	elder or senior vassal, who might deputize in the daimyo's absence
kerai	retainers of a daimyo
koshō	pages or squires
maku	curtains that enclosed a general's field headquarters
mon	family badge
nobori	long vertical banner
rōnin	masterless samurai
samurai	warrior (feudal or retained)
sashimono	a samurai's personal identifying back-standard or flag
taishō	general, tactical commander in battle
tozama	'outer' lords, who submitted to a daimyo only after being defeated by him or witnessing his victory over others

DEDICATION
To my four-legged friend Buster, with whom I frequently discussed this project during our walks together.

AUTHOR'S NOTE
This book is intended as a companion piece to my previous titles in the Osprey Elite series, ELI 125 & 128: *Samurai Commanders (I)* and *(II)*, and ELI 82: *Samurai Heraldry*. By looking at the *hatamoto* as individuals it completes the story of the Japanese *daimyo* and those who fought beside him, and should be read in conjunction with my other book, BTO 36: *Samurai Armies 1467–1649*, which provides detailed numerical information about the armies in which the *hatamoto* played such a unique and crucial role.

Some of the famous episodes of loyalty and self-sacrifice by *hatamoto* in the service of their *daimyo* will already be familiar to some readers, and to avoid unnecessary repetition from my earlier books I have also included here a number of instances from the lesser-known exploits of the *daimyo* of northern Japan, whose lives and careers I was able to study in detail during my tenure as Visiting Professor of Japanese Studies at Akita International University. Here, in works such as '*Ou Eikei Gunki*', which deals with the civil wars of the northern *daimyo* between 1560 and 1603, we find some striking examples of *hatamoto* in action. These include a few remarkable events undertaken after their lords had been deposed or even killed, all of which are prime examples of the loyalty that was implied by the title of someone who stood 'beneath the flag'.

ACKNOWLEDGEMENTS
I wish to thank the staff of Akita Prefectural Library and of Akita International University Library for their guidance and help in supplying these materials. Till Weber, of the University of the Ryūkyūs, also made some very helpful suggestions during the preparation of this work.

ARTIST'S NOTE
Readers may care to note that the original paintings from which the colour plates in this book were prepared are available for private sale. All reproduction copyright whatsoever is retained by the Publishers. All enquiries should be addressed to:

Scorpio Gallery, PO Box 475, Hailsham, East Sussex BN27 2SL, UK

The Publishers regret that they can enter into no correspondence upon this matter.

EDITOR'S NOTE
To avoid confusion over the use of italics in this text: note that generally only Japanese nouns that may be unfamiliar are italicized in the body text. Very commonly used terms – e.g. *samurai, daimyo, ashigaru* – are italicized only at their first use, as is *hatamoto* itself. Italicized words between apostrophes – e.g. '*Shinchōko-ki*' – are the titles of documentary sources.

CONTENTS

'THOSE BENEATH THE FLAG'   4
Heavenly generals . Defensible space . Loyalty relationships . Structure and function
Hatamoto in time of peace

HORSE GUARDS: ORGANIZATION AND ROLES   25

FOOT GUARDS: ORGANIZATION AND ROLES   38

HATAMOTO IN ACTION   43
The northern hatamoto, 1591–1603 . War by delegation . The Satake hatamoto at Osaka, 1614

BIBLIOGRAPHY & FURTHER READING   63

INDEX   64

HATAMOTO
SAMURAI HORSE AND FOOT GUARDS 1540–1724

'THOSE BENEATH THE FLAG'

The word *hatamoto* has the literal meaning of 'beneath the flag', because it was directly underneath the flags and battle standards of the *daimyo* (Japan's feudal lords) that one would have found the *samurai* warriors who bore this

Satō Tadanobu, one of Minamoto Yoshitsune's four Shitennō or 'heavenly kings' and the prototype for the loyalty and self-sacrifice demanded from a hatamoto. In this woodblock print Tadanobu provides a rearguard to allow Yoshitsune to escape through the heavy snow on Mount Yoshino.

most noble of titles. They made up the daimyo's mounted and foot guards; served on his general staff, to plan strategy and to supervise his military administration; or provided immediate personal services to their lord, of which the most important of all was the shared duty of protecting his person. Every hatamoto, therefore, was to some extent a true guardsman who was willing to throw himself in front of his lord when danger threatened – which was no more than would be expected from these bravest and most loyal of all samurai warriors.

The battlefield exploits of the hatamoto provide some of the most stirring episodes in samurai history, but not all were completely successful in their fundamental role of guarding their lord. In these pages a handful of disasters will provide examples of hatamoto failing to save the life of their daimyo, but these incidents are outnumbered by the successful feats of loyalty and self-sacrifice accomplished by other hatamoto, whose bravery and military skills ensured the future of many a lord's house in its moment of darkest peril.

HEAVENLY GENERALS

The notion of guarding and protecting one's master is a concept that even predates the first use of the word *samurai* (literally, 'one who serves') to denote a Japanese fighting man, from whose ranks the elite hatamoto were to emerge. The earliest samurai were employed as imperial guards to the Emperors of Japan during the Nara Period (AD 710–794), and contemporary illustrations exist that show them wearing flowing robes, carrying bows, and riding horses as they carry out their duties. It is with the rise to power and prominence of influential samurai families such as the Minamoto and Taira, and their rivalry during the Gempei Wars of 1180–85, that we see elite samurai acting as personal bodyguards not only to the emperor but also to their own leaders, most of whom were the heads of their clans. In some prominent cases these guards, the forerunners of the hatamoto, consisted of four named individuals who were collectively referred to as the Shitennō, the 'four heavenly kings', by analogy with the four great kings of heaven who protect the world from attacks by demons, each with his own responsibility for one of the four cardinal points. Thus Minamoto Yoshitsune (1159–89), the greatest general of the Gempei Wars, was served by four loyal Shitennō named Ise Yoshimori, Suruga Jirō and the brothers Satō Tsuginobu and Satō Tadanobu.

We can read of Yoshitsune's 'heavenly kings', otherwise known as 'heavenly generals', in the epic *gunkimono* (war tale) called '*Heike Monogatari*', where

Using the ancient terminology, Sakakibara Yasumasa was one of the four Shitennō ('heavenly kings') of Tokugawa Ieyasu. Here he sits under his personal banner.

Throughout samurai history the headquarters of a general on the battlefield was marked by the erection of an enclosure called the *maku*, formed from heavy curtains suspended from poles. In this very early example in the style of the 12th century we also see the flags used by the samurai, in the form of streamers hung from crosspieces. To 'stand under these flags' is the origin of the word *hatamoto*.

they are to be found in action at the battle of Yashima in 1184 in a classic instance of their role. There, together with Yoshitsune's companion the monk Benkei and other brave warriors, the Shitennō form a line in front of Yoshitsune to receive the arrows being shot at him. This succeeds in saving Yoshitsune's life, but one arrow strikes Satō Tsuginobu and 'pierced him through from the left shoulder to the right armpit, and, no longer able to sit his horse, [he] fell to the ground.' Yoshitsune orders Tsuginobu to be carried to the rear, and as soon as it is safe to do so he takes the hand of his faithful follower. The dying Tsuginobu expresses his regret that he will not live to see his lord come into his own, but is happy to know that future generations will be told of his loyalty; 'to have died instead of my lord at the fight on the beach of Yashima in Sanuki, in the war of the Genji and Heike, will be my pride in this life and something to remember on the dark road of death'.

Tsuginobu's brother Satō Tadanobu survived the battle of Yashima and continued to serve Minamoto Yoshitsune almost to the very end, accompanying him during the early stages of his wanderings to escape the wrath of Yoshitsune's jealous brother Minamoto Yoritomo. In the mountains of Yoshino, as related in '*Gikeiki*', Satō Tadanobu offers to fight a rearguard action while Yoshitsune escapes, and makes the suggestion that he should pretend to be Yoshitsune until the very last moment. Yoshitsune reluctantly agrees, and the two men exchange armour, although the writer of '*Gikeiki*' stresses that this is not so much to aid the deception as to provide the brave Tadanobu with a better defensive harness. The plan succeeds, and Tadanobu survives; he escapes to Kyoto, but there he is eventually tracked down by his enemies. Making his last stand, Tadanobu is forced to defend himself from a surprise attack using only a playing board for the game of *go* before reaching for his sword to commit *seppuku* (ritual suicide). '*Gikeiki*' concludes with the death of Yoshitsune at the battle of Koromogawa in 1189, where he is introduced to two boys who turn out to be the sons of the Satō brothers and who will continue the traditions of their fathers. Yoshitsune then fights to the last, and is shielded from the enemy by a wall of loyal samurai guards while he too commits suicide.

In these stories, although naturally somewhat embroidered by legend, we see encapsulated the values of a lord's personal guard that were to be re-echoed for centuries to come in the role of the hatamoto. There is, first, the attitude of complete loyalty that makes a hatamoto instinctively move into the path of an arrow or a bullet intended for his lord. Then there is the desire to sacrifice his own life in a rearguard action so that his lord may survive, even to the extent of disguising himself as the lord – a ruse that came to be known as the *kagemusha* ('shadow warrior'). Finally, we see the hereditary principle of service being passed on down the generations.

DEFENSIBLE SPACE

The first use of the word *hatamoto* appears during the Sengoku Period (1467–1615). This was Japan's 'Age of Warring States', when scores of minor daimyo seized power for themselves in their immediate localities and fought each other until, during the mid-16th century, a comparative handful of 'super-daimyo' competed with each other on a grand scale before Japan was finally reunified. The original meaning of hatamoto, however, referred less to the men and more to the place where they gathered. This area 'beneath the flag' was most precisely defined when a general (who was usually the daimyo himself, but might be a highly trusted follower) set up his field headquarters on the march or in immediate preparation for battle.

Even though the location of the *honjin* (headquarters) might be just a bare hillock or a clearing in a forest, its defensible space was defined by being enclosed within a rectangle of heavy cloth curtains. The curtains (*maku*) were suspended from ropes on stout iron poles hammered into the ground, and bore the daimyo's *mon* (badge) in large, bold designs. When the army moved on the *maku* went with it, the poles being strapped to pack saddles and the curtains themselves being folded neatly into boxes on the backs of other packhorses. So common was the use of the *maku* that Japan's first military government – which was set up by the first shogun, Minamoto Yoritomo, in 1192 – was called the *bakufu*, or 'government from within the field curtains'.

Seated within his *maku* with his hatamoto, Tokugawa Ieyasu directs the battle of Sekigahara, 1600, in this detail from a painted screen in the Watanabe Collection, Tottori. (In fact, on this occasion Ieyasu is believed to have worn the quasi-European armour illustrated in Plate E.) When setting out on a long-planned campaign an army might take the means to augument the *maku* into a more solid temporary defence like a Roman *castrum*, with fences and ditches, but even these could be breached by determined attackers, and depended on the human defenders.

Tokugawa Ieyasu's guards surrounding him during his advance at the battle of the Anegawa, 1570. This is a detail from a modern screen painting done in traditional style, on display in a museum commemorating the Asai family near Nagahama.

Even during the peaceful Edo Period (1603–1868) the government of the shogunate was called the Bakufu in a clear reference to its military origins.

The area within a typical *maku* was by no means elaborately furnished. Folding camp stools would be provided for the daimyo and his staff officers, but a wooden mantlet placed on top of two stools would have sufficed as a table. The only other structures present might include long wooden frames into which the shafts of the flags and standards would be slotted. Numerous long, narrow vertical banners *(nobori)*, suspended from bamboo shafts with a horizontal crosspiece, would be arranged behind the lord on three sides, making the field headquarters visible from a considerable distance. Flags *(hata)* provide the origin of the word for both the space they defined and the men who stood beneath them.

The flags of earlier leaders such as Yoshitsune were simple streamers carried by a mounted standard-bearer to indicate the general's presence, but by about 1560 a trend had emerged for the focal point of a samurai army arrayed for battle to be not merely a plain flag but the *o uma jirushi* or 'great horse insignia'. This battle standard was indeed in some cases a large flag, but was in most instances a striking three-dimensional object made from wood, cloth

A **ODA NOBUNAGA'S RED AND BLACK HORO HORSE GUARDS, 1568**

The elite bodyguards of a lord's hatamoto were his small troop of Horse Guards, but when Oda Nobunaga moved against Mitsukuriyama Castle in 1568 he – unusually – risked his in battle by giving them the task of leading the vanguard in the assault. His 20-strong Horse Guards were divided into two squads, each distinguished by wearing on their backs either a red or a black *horo*, a balloon-like framed cloak. Two members of each squad also sported 'angel's wings' with their *horo*. Here we see Asai Shimpachi (**1**) of the Red Horo Horse Guards with golden wings, and Matsuoka Kurojirō (**2**) of the Black squad with silver wings, leading the charge; they are closely followed by the other two 'winged' samurai, Maeda Toshiie of the Red Guards and Kawajiri Hidetaka of the Black Guards. The suits of armour they wear are of *mogami-dō* style, i.e. composed of separate hinged sections each made from a series of solid lacquered plates laced together. Asai Shimpachi wears a gold-lacquered *maedate* (helmet badge) in the shape of a rising sun, while Matsuoka Kurojirō's is a representation of the sword of the deity Fudō.

or papier-mâché. Within a leader's *honjin* it would be mounted in a heavy, secure frame. When on the move it would be strapped onto a standard-bearer's back, with two other 'colour guardsmen' to assist him with his burden; these would hold onto ropes to steady the contrivance as it waved in the wind.

The presence of the curtains, standards and flags rendered the *honjin* very conspicuous, but a *maku* was never intended to be anything more than a temporary structure and had almost no defensive capability in itself: it provided privacy, but little more. A few unobtrusive spyholes cut at waist level, and perhaps the erection of a rough wooden palisade around the outside, were the limits to the possibilities for making cloth curtains into a defensive wall; the wall within the *maku* was human, provided by the hatamoto.

Needless to say, a similar vigilance was required when a daimyo was on the move. His advance would be preceded by scouts, and as he rode towards battle his horse guards could provide a moving shield. When in retreat the situation became much more acute, and we read of several instances of hatamoto risking all to cover their lord's withdrawal, just as Satō Tadanobu did for Yoshitsune. During the battle of the Anegawa, Nobunaga's enemy Asakura Kagetake was completely surrounded in a furious mêlée. It was essential that the Asakura army withdraw to the northern bank of the river, and a certain samurai called Makara Jurōzaemon Naotaka, a hatamoto of the Asakura, volunteered to cover their retreat. He was apparently a giant of a man who carried a *nōdachi*, a sword with a blade over 5ft long. Like the samurai of old whose stories he would have been told as a child, Makara bellowed out his name. His challenge was first accepted by a vassal of the Tokugawa called Ogasawara Nagatada, whom Makara killed. He was

In this lively modern painting on display at the site of the battle of the Anegawa, we see Makara Jurōzaemon Naotaka, a hatamoto of the Asakura, who volunteered to cover their retreat. Makara Jurōzaemon was a giant of a samurai who carried a sword with a blade more than 5ft long.

then joined by his eldest son Makara Jurōsaburō Naomoto, and together father and son faced repeated attacks by Tokugawa samurai as the Asakura withdrew. Makara was dragged off his horse by a warrior using a cross-bladed spear and decapitated, and soon afterwards his son was also killed, but their sacrifice had not been in vain; their rearguard action had allowed the Asakura army to retreat in good order, even though they were then pursued for a considerable distance.

LOYALTY RELATIONSHIPS

As the hatamoto had the simultaneous responsibilities of defending the daimyo and assisting him in the discharge of his governance and leadership they may be seen by analogy as his 'household brigade', and indeed in Japan the notion of 'household' was central to understanding their origins and the social structure within their ranks. The general term for a daimyo's followers was *kerai*, a word usually translated as 'retainers' by analogy with feudal Europe. Historically, great emphasis was placed on the closeness of the blood relationship between a lord and his retainers within the *kashindan* (vassal band) formed from them – a group that in times of strife functioned under the name of his *gundan* (war band). Political marriage liaisons were commonplace in making up a *kashindan*, as was the trading of mature sons through adoption, and in almost all records of *kashindan* we find a separate unit of close kinsmen where the names of the daimyo's sons and brothers are listed. Yet this does not necessarily imply that

ABOVE LEFT
Endō Naotsugu provides a rare example of a samurai succeeding in penetrating the *maku* of an enemy general. Determined to kill Oda Nobunaga at the battle of the Anegawa in 1570, Naotsugu smeared his face with blood, removed his identifying flag, and approached the *maku* carrying a severed head that he said he was going to present to his master Nobunaga. Challenged by a vigilant hatamoto, he was overcome by Nobunaga's guards.

ABOVE RIGHT
Sakai Tadatsugu, a hatamoto of the Tokugawa, is shown here wearing a *sashimono* of a model skull at the battle of Nagashino, 1575.

A loyal hatamoto stood under his lord's standard for life, as shown by this grizzled old veteran whose hair has turned grey in his lord's service.

these individuals were his most loyal followers. In some cases the reverse was true, so that the inclusion of their names in a distinct section might be seen more as a means of surveillance and control. Oda Nobunaga (1534–82) initially rose to power in Owari province by overcoming rivals from within his own family. His successor Toyotomi Hideyoshi (1536–98) was to dispose of his nephew and adopted heir Hidetsugu when rebellion was suspected; and Tokugawa Ieyasu (1542–1616), the man who finally achieved the reunification of Japan and whose family was to rule the country for 250 years, even oversaw the killing of one of his own sons.

A better guarantee of loyalty to a daimyo than shared blood was the swearing of an oath of fealty, and the bonds created by this solemn undertaking between a lord and his vassals could last for generations. In some cases this oath was also demanded from relatives; yet even such a solemn pledge was not foolproof, and an examination of the early career of Tokugawa Ieyasu reveals how precarious these crucial bonds of loyalty could be, particularly during the initial stages of their formation.

In 1563 Mikawa province, where Ieyasu was building up the strength of his retainer band and taking into his service those individuals who were to be his hatamoto for decades to come, was a region divided by competing loyalties. The long-standing relationship between Ieyasu's Matsudaira family and their own former overlords, the Imagawa, had been shattered by the defeat and death of Imagawa Yoshimoto when his own hatamoto had failed him at Okehazama in 1560. Ieyasu was thereby effectively freed from his former obligation and was moving towards a formal alliance with Oda Nobunaga, the victor at Okehazama. Some of Ieyasu's followers saw this as indicating a lack of loyalty to their old master's heir, and objected to the move. However, a more serious rift was caused by local religious affiliations, because some local warriors were forced to choose between their successful and ambitious young lord and the competing demands of their faith.

Mikawa province was an important location for the adherents of the Honganji, the main branch of the Jōdo Shinshū ('True Pure Land' sect), which had broken away from the original 'Pure Land' sect of Buddhism to which Tokugawa Ieyasu belonged. Followers of the True Pure Land organized themselves in armies, the famous Ikkō-ikki, based around the defensible

Shibata Katsuie (1530–83) was the *karō* (chief retainer) of Oda Nobunaga, enjoying a degree of trust as a hatamoto that Nobunaga did not extend to many of his own relatives. Here we see Katsuie performing his most famous act of loyalty, in 1570 during the siege of Chokōji Castle, which he defended until starvation and thirst promised defeat. Knowing the garrison were unlikely to survive, he smashed the water jars and led his samurai out in a death-defying charge so vigorous that he scattered the besiegers and saved the castle.

Umezu Noritada (1571–1630) became *karō* of the Satake family after fighting fiercely at the battle of Imafuku in 1614, one of the actions in which the surroundings of Osaka Castle were seized by the Tokugawa. This 'Yellow Devil of the Satake clan' is shown here in a hanging scroll owned by Akita Prefectural Archives. His flag is a white temple bell on black, and he wears a yellow *jinbaori* surcoat.

communities associated with their *jinaichō* (temple towns). These centres wielded a similar economic power to that of the rising daimyo, and added a further level of complication to the question of where a samurai's loyalty might lie.

In 1563 fighting broke out between Tokugawa Ieyasu and the *monto* (disciples) of the Honganji. Two separate incidents appear to have occurred, of which the first was at the Jōgūji temple when one of Ieyasu's samurai seized the temple's rice to feed his followers. The *monto* attacked this man's castle, retrieved the rice and barricaded themselves into their fortified temple. When Ieyasu sent messengers to enquire about the incident they were summarily beheaded. In the second clash a samurai attacked the house of a merchant who owed him money in the temple town associated with the Honshōji temple. Ieyasu launched a raid against the Honshōji, which was resisted forcibly.

The fighting between Ieyasu and the Honganji continued until 1564 and included at least one major battle at a place called Azukizaka. The accounts of this engagement well illustrate the divided loyalties suffered by some of Ieyasu's lower-ranking samurai, of which the most vivid example is that of a certain Tsuchiya Chokiri, who had taken the side of his religion as a *monto* even though he was also a follower of Ieyasu. It was only when he saw Ieyasu in desperate straits during the fighting (he had been hit by two bullets) that Chokiri decided where his true allegiance lay, and turned against the Ikkō-ikki until he himself was killed.

For Ieyasu's higher-ranking retainers the choice of ultimate loyalty had been a more considered one made before the event. The head of the main branch of the Honda family, Honda Tadakatsu (1548–1610), abandoned the schismatic True Pure Land sect for the orthodox Pure Land, and went on to serve under Ieyasu's standard in all his battles. By contrast, his kinsman Honda Masanobu (1539–1617), from the junior branch of the family, chose initially to fight for the Ikkō-ikki and only submitted to Ieyasu after their defeat. He was, nevertheless, to rise to prominence in later life as one of Ieyasu's closest advisers. The extensive Honda clan had thus effectively hedged their bets over which side might win. The Watanabe family, under their leader Watanabe Hanzō Moritsuna (1542–1620) – who was to be nicknamed 'Hanzō the Spear' – did not break ranks at all when they decided to support the Ikkō-ikki side, and in the following extract from '*Watanabe Chūemon oboegaki*' we see two families who were to supply future hatamoto of Tokugawa Ieyasu fighting on opposite sides:

Okubo Yoichirō came out of his castle towards Hanzō, who was loosing arrows at a furious pace. When Hanzō grabbed his spear, he made Yoichirō retreat towards the fortified gate. Hanzō pursued him, saying, 'I'll throw this at you and run you through with it!', but the spear did not even reach Yoichirō's body, and he retreated into the castle. Hanzō then went back to the temple.

Tokugawa Ieyasu eventually overcame the Ikkō-ikki activists in his province, and from that time onwards considerations arising from religious beliefs do not appear to have been an important hindrance in the development of his *kashindan*. What mattered most of all was the quality of loyalty and military skill, although we do find considerable evidence that a daimyo also valued common sense on the part of a hatamoto. In 1574 Gamō Ujisato (1557–96), who was married to Nobunaga's daughter and had captured his first castle at the age of 13, took immense risks to bring back an enemy's head; instead of receiving praise from his father-in-law he was criticized for his recklessness – good hatamoto should never get themselves killed wastefully.

STRUCTURE & FUNCTION

The *karō*

The most senior rank attainable by a man who had entered a daimyo's service through pledging an oath of fealty was that of *karō*, the 'family elder' or senior vassal among the hatamoto, who was frequently more trusted than a lord's blood relatives. It is noticeable that within the structure of Oda Nobunaga's *kashindan* in about 1570 one branch contains only the names of Nobunaga's sons and brothers, while the other branch, in which the important senior retainers and virtually the whole of Nobunaga's army are listed, is controlled through the person of Nobunaga's *karō* Shibata Katsuie (1530–83). During the Edo Period, the long time of peace created by the re-establishment of the shogunate by Tokugawa Ieyasu, if a daimyo was absent from his castle town on official duties for the shogun his *karō* was left in sole charge of the domain and enjoyed great trust.

An important role within the hatamoto was played by the officials who acted as *yūhitsu* (secretaries). They came under the jurisdiction of the *metsuke* (inspectors), who had responsibility for investigating battlefield conduct. In this detail from the painted screen depicting the Summer Campaign of Osaka we see a secretary keeping a tally of the severed heads that have been delivered as trophies.

One example of the contrasting roles of the *karō* during war and peace is provided by the Satake family of the Kubota *han* (fief) in modern Akita prefecture. In 1614 the daimyo Satake Yoshinobu (1570–1633) fought for the Tokugawa side at the battle of Imafuku, one of the crucial actions whereby the besieging Tokugawa army took control of the outlying positions around Osaka Castle. Shibue Naizen Masateru, the *karō* of the Satake family, was fully involved in the fighting at Imafuku and was killed in a mêlée so confused that it was some time before even his immediate followers learned of his death. (One of his *gokenin* or 'housemen', Tosai Jubei, only learned of it when he was on his way out of battle to present a severed head to his master. In his grief Jubei threw the head into the rice fields.) After the Satake army had returned to Akita the position of *karō* was given to Umezu Noritada (1571–1630), another member of the Satake hatamoto, whose vigorous fighting at Imafuku had earned him the nickname of the 'Yellow Devil of the Satake clan'. During the subsequent peaceful Edo Period the warrior Noritada continued to serve the Satake until his death in 1630 at the age of 59, providing a classic example of a loyal and dedicated peacetime administrator. The 'Yellow Devil's' younger brother Umezu Masakage, a noted diarist, also held several important positions within the Satake hierarchy until his own death in 1633.

The two examples of Oda Nobunaga and Satake Yoshinobu provide cases where a daimyo appointed just one *karō* to act as his trusted deputy. Other lords had more than one *karō*, and other titles – such as *shukurō* or *roshin* – may also be found in reference to senior retainers. All imply a very senior status for someone who has pledged a lifetime's allegiance to the daimyo both on the battlefield and in civil life. Yet whatever degree of delegation a daimyo may have made to his hatamoto, the wise lord kept his own counsel. When Tokugawa Ieyasu was conducting the siege of Kanie castle in 1584 his generals reported to him that reinforcements were arriving in the castle by boat. To their surprise Ieyasu ordered them not to intervene, and he would not tell them the reason why he had decided on such an unusual course of action. Later Ieyasu seized all the enemy boats and cut off the flow of supplies completely, and the castle surrendered earlier than would have been expected because of the number crammed into it. Ieyasu clearly felt the need to maintain secrecy over his intentions even among his inner circle.

Whatever the origin of their vassal status or their rank they held, the hatamoto were the men who, on the battlefield, would be required to channel

B **KURODA NAGASAMA AND TŌDŌ TAKATORA, 1592**

The two daimyo are depicted holding a formal council of war in Korea, at the field headquarters of Kuroda Nagamasa (**1**). Nagamasa (1568–1623) commanded the Third Division of the Japanese army during Hideyoshi's invasion, and Tōdō Takatora (1556–1630) (**2**) was responsible for naval transport. Within the ranks of the hatamoto were several samurai who had specific functions with regard to the welfare, safety and convenience of their daimyo. It was customary for a lord not to put on his elaborate helmet until quite late in a battle; otherwise the helmets were carried by helmet-bearers who were selected from the ranks of the hatamoto for their outstanding bravery, because the helmet acted as a personal identifier for the daimyo and could thus attract the fiercest fire. Nagamasa's helmet (**1a**) is ornamented with enormous gold-lacquered wooden water-buffalo horns, while Takatora's bearer carries a helmet (**2a**) described as being in 'the Chinese style', with a simple bowl set off by two huge spear-blades projecting at the sides. Each general is also accompanied by an ashigaru carrying his *ko uma jirushi* (lesser standard), the smaller of the two standards maintained by a daimyo's army. Kuroda Nagamasa's standard (**1b**) has a series of small golden flags on a tree-like framework, while Tōdō Takatora's is a golden umbrella with a red fringe (**2b**). In the background we see the *maku* bearing the large Kuroda *mon* (badge) on a blue background.

The taking of an enemy's head was the surest proof of duty done. In this modern painting Mōri Motonari ritually insults the head of Sue Harukata after the battle of Miyajima, 1555; this was the famous battle that polluted the sacred island and required Shinto rites of purification.

whatever administrative and leadership talents they possessed into military roles within the 'household brigade'. Such talents might be exercised as *taishō* (generals) in command of the tactical units of mounted or foot samurai and the specialist squads of *ashigaru* (common footsoldiers) armed with matchlock arquebus, spear and bow. These 'troops of the line' were organized in units usually called *kumi* (written as '*-gumi*' when used as a suffix), as distinct from the normal use of the term *ban* (guard) for the units within the hatamoto.

Other members of the hatamoto, termed *bugyō* (commissioners), had a wider remit than simply leading men into battle, and bore responsibility for logistics, ordnance and support services of various kinds. Yet all these 'staff officers' also stood guard 'beneath the flag' inside the *maku* as members of the hatamoto, prepared to die for their lord, and later years would immortalize the names of senior retainers by such titles as the 'Twenty-Four Generals of the Takeda' or the 'Sixteen Generals of the Tokugawa'. Lists of the Takeda senior retainers in fact show a variation among 33 names in all, as old age and death in battle claimed victims from their ranks. Takeda Shingen set as his criteria of excellence the possession of good judgement, a readiness to carry out punishments, and the achievement of victory in battle – a neat summary of the qualities of the ideal hatamoto.

The *bugyō*

The *bugyō* (a word usually translated as 'commissioners' in wartime and 'magistrates' in peacetime) were the general staff officers within a daimyo's army who provided, among other services, strategic and tactical advice. Within a *maku* they were to be found seated in council with the daimyo. Some *bugyō*, as noted in a list for the Onodera family, acted 'without portfolio', while others had specific responsibilities. Titles vary from daimyo to daimyo, but usually included an *ikusa bugyō* (commissioner for the army) otherwise known as the *sōbugyō* (overall commissioner), who was equivalent to a field marshal. It was to this man that a daimyo might delegate strategic and tactical decisions; if necessary he would also take complete charge of military operations in the absence of his lord. This was quite common practice, and we read of many operations being conducted by a trusted hatamoto – sometimes a daimyo's relative, but more often than not a highly experienced senior retainer.

The *maku bugyō* or *jinba bugyō* was responsible for the transport, siting and erection of the field headquarters, and the duties of the *hata bugyō* (flag commissioner) included not only the supply and organization of flags but their proper use for signalling on the battlefield. The *yari bugyō* (spear commissioner) oversaw the administration of all matters relating to those weapons, including not only the specialist spear squads of the 'line troops' but also the use of spears by the samurai. Likewise, there were a *yumi bugyō* (archery commissioner) and *teppō bugyō* (arquebus commissioner) responsible for the bow and firearms units. The *yoroi bugyō* (armour commissioner) saw to the procurement and distribution of armour for the entire army.

The *shodōgu bugyō* (equipment commissioner) played a similar role with regard to all other items of an army's equipment, but we cannot simply call him the 'quartermaster general', since he was not responsible for the commissariat. That fell to the *hyōrō bugyō* (provisions commissioner), who administered the purchase of sufficient rations, foraging, storage and transport of all food for the troops and fodder for the horses. Serving under him would be the *konida bugyō* (packhorse commissioner) who supervised the transport on horseback or in carts of army food supplies. These would then be handed over to the *daidokoro bugyō* (kitchen commissioner), who was responsible for the supply of meals from field kitchens. A separate *fune bugyō* (boat commissioner) took charge of everything relating to transport by water.

The *yokome*

Holding a position equivalent in prestige to the *bugyō* were the *ikusa metsuke* (army superintendents) otherwise known as the *yokome* (inspectors). These men combined roles analogous to those of European provosts and military judges with that of heralds. In peacetime they had a disciplinary function, and on the battlefield this extended to overseeing the behaviour – good and bad – of individual samurai. As well as identifying instances of bravery and cowardice, they would investigate and assess as true or false any ambiguous claims of glorious achievement; we may infer that the

Katakura Kagetsuna was an outstanding example of the loyal hatamoto, who served Date Masamune and kept the castle of Shiroishi. His personal banner also bears a temple bell motif, like that of Umezu Noritada.

samurai obsession with individual prowess kept them very busy. If necessary they would preside over what were virtually military courts of enquiry, when exploits were discussed and differences settled. Their other tasks included the counting of heads and the identification both of the victim and the victor. This was often done in the field, when the traditional head-viewing ceremony was performed immediately after the battle had been won (the occasion on which a miscalculation cost Imagawa Yoshimoto dearly at Okehazama – see below, 'Nobunaga's Horse Guards').

HATAMOTO IN TIME OF PEACE

Tokugawa Ieyasu was the ultimate victor in the civil wars of the Sengoku Period, and following the battle of Sekigahara in 1600 he re-established the shogunate and became the first shogun of the Tokugawa dynasty. As the Tokugawa Bakufu increased its grip on Japan, so the term hatamoto began to lose its primary military meaning, evolving to denote both the men who were now members of the shogun's standing army and the administrators of his government. To some extent, of course, all hatamoto theoretically performed both roles, and every man so honoured had to keep himself in readiness for battle. Because of the total dominance of the Tokugawa family this meant that they were in all but name both the 'Japanese national army' and the civil servants of the central government.

At the highest level of the Tokugawa civil service stood a handful of daimyo called the *fudai*. These men were hereditary retainers of the Tokugawa who had entered Ieyasu's service before his victory at Sekigahara. All controlled *han* of their own with a value of not less than 10,000 *koku* of rice (one *koku* was the amount regarded as necessary to feed one man for one year). Below them, with territories producing annual incomes of between 9,500 and 100 *koku*, were the men who were now called the hatamoto. These were entitled to at least one personal audience with the shogun; by 1635, the earliest date for which reliable figures are available, their number stood at

In this hanging scroll in the Memorial Hall of the battle of Nagashino we see 'the Twenty-Four Generals of Takeda Shingen'. The term is not a contemporary one, but in Japanese culture the use of numerical categories to denote the most loyal or most senior members of a lord's hatamoto is not uncommon.

One of the most important roles of the hatamoto during the peaceful Edo Period was to escort the daimyo during his periodic visits to Edo to pay his respects to the shogun.

about 5,000 men. Because of their obligation to supply troops for the shogun in addition to their own personal service, a call to arms of the hatamoto would have resulted in an army of about 80,000 men. This figure included those who occupied the third tier of the hierarchy, below the hatamoto, who were called *yoriki* or *gokenin;* these commanded the 'line infantry' squads of *dōshin* or ashigaru footsoldiers within the Tokugawa army. Theoretically the *yoriki* were men worth less than 100 *koku* annually, but there was some overlap between the two categories at the lower levels of hatamoto status.

Any hatamoto who lived during the first quarter of the 17th century would have experienced a considerable change in his role as his career progressed, and some achieved high promotion through participation in the final battles of the Tokugawa at Osaka in 1614–15 and Shimabara in 1638. For example, Uemura Iemasa (1589–1650) rose from being the son of a *rōnin* (masterless samurai) to become a daimyo. Iemasa's father had died in 1599 after being employed to fight in Ieyasu's wars, so at the age of 11 Iemasa inherited his modest stipend. Tokugawa Hidetada, Ieyasu's heir, made Iemasa one of his *koshō* (pages – see below under 'Foot Guards'), and by 1608 Iemasa had become an *okachi kashira* (captain of footsoldiers). He distinguished himself at the siege of Osaka when he led a patrol through enemy lines, and in 1625 was made a *kashira* in the Great Guard. In 1633 he received a castle of his own and the status of daimyo.

The Tokugawa Bakufu disapproved of any hatamoto forming too close a relationship with the farmers working the land allotted to him. In the past such links had led to rebellion, so as time went by the actual ownership of land was replaced by the receipt of a stipend of rice equivalent to the land's worth. This was a pattern copied for the hatamoto retainers of the daimyo, both of the *fudai* (inner lords) and the *tozama* (outer lords) – the latter being the ones who had submitted to Ieyasu only after his triumph in 1600 and thus enjoyed only the qualified trust of the shogun. Many daimyo therefore withdrew the hatamoto of less than 500 *koku* from their lands and offered them a fixed stipend instead. These men would probably then choose to live within the garrisons of the castle towns, of which the most important establishment of all was mighty Edo – modern Tokyo – the seat of the Tokugawa shogunate.

The shogun's own hatamoto lived within the concentric rings of defences around Edo Castle, where they were joined on a regular basis by the troops of provincial daimyo when they visited Edo to pay their respects to the shogun. The 'alternate attendance system', whereby a lord's family lived in Edo but he was normally based in his own castle town, was a very sophisticated hostage system. At intervals dependent upon the daimyo's geographical distance from Edo he would visit the capital with a large military retinue, and live there for several months. Each daimyo had a particular city block assigned to him, and behind its heavy gates, thick walls and dark latticed windows his rule held sway as if he were at home in his castle town. Outside those walls he and his men were under the control of the Tokugawa hatamoto, who were required to police their districts as part of their duties in return for the grant of a stipend. The day-to-day practical policing function was delegated to the *yoriki*, who used the *dōshin* as the 'policemen on the beat'.

The main means of physical control within the samurai quarters of Edo was through the maintenance of guard posts near many street corners, the forerunners of the *koban* (police stations) of today. In the areas of the city reserved for commoners the streets were gated, but in samurai districts these guard houses were the only centres of control. A law of 1629 stipulated that men were to be sent out from the guard house if any 'violent, wounded or suspicious person is sighted'. The guards' functions included taking into custody anyone who had caused bloodshed, but also helping anyone who had had an accident, aiding lost children, the disposal of abandoned corpses and even the collection of rubbish. Although the jurisdiction of a visiting daimyo did not extend beyond his own compound, his hatamoto were required to mount guard duty just like the shogun's own men, but if a fight occurred outside the gates of a compound the men involved were not to be taken inside it but to the nearest guard post. A notice issued by the Bakufu to the daimyo of Tosa makes it clear that:

> If a person is cut down with a sword in front of the compound, hunt the assailant down. If he will not surrender his sword, you may kill him. If he does surrender his sword you may hand him over to the magistrate's office.

The control of such mundane incidents was now among the main functions of the hatamoto whose ancestors had once literally stood 'beneath the flag', because warfare had now all but ceased. Yet vigilance was the key, and assignment to one of the military units in the shogun's army did not limit a hatamoto to a purely bureaucratic role; he still had to maintain himself as a battle-ready samurai and to demonstrate personal proficiency in the martial

---

C: TOYOTOMI HIDEYOSHI'S HORSE GUARDS, 1582

Like his former master Oda Nobunaga, Toyotomi Hideyoshi (1536–98) was served by an elite guards unit, and from 1581 onwards this had grown from its single company of Yellow Horo Horse Guards to incorporate two more mounted units: the Red Horo Guards, and the Great Horo Guards (otherwise known as the War Fan Guards). Here we see a representative from each of the three units at the time of the battle of Yamazaki in 1582, the victory by which Hideyoshi secured his succession over Nobunaga's family. The Red Horo Guard (**1**) is dismounted, and in addition to his red *horo* displays a large gold-lacquered crescent moon rising from his *sashimono* holder. The Yellow Horo Guard (**2**) wears a golden-yellow *horo* of similar size, while the Great Horo Guard (**3**) has an extra-large yellow *horo*; this was purely ceremonial and would not be worn in combat, when the golden *uchiwa* (war fan), shown here displayed above the large *horo*, would have sufficed.

The reality of life for a hatamoto during the peaceful Edo Period was the monotony of office work, captured here in a life-sized diorama in the reconstructed samurai quarter of Matsumae Castle on the island of Hokkaido.

arts. His daily duties were therefore those of conventional peacetime soldiering: standing guard, accompanying the shogun on his trips out of Edo, taking part in parades, as well as performing some administrative role usually concerned with building construction or repair. Detailed regulations covered their times of guard duty, their dress and appearance, and the areas of the castle where they had to operate. A considerable amount of effort also had to be devoted to the ritual of visits and gift-giving to superiors that arose from the hatamoto's place in the Confucian-inspired hierarchy of the Tokugawa shogunate.

In the Edo Period the average Tokugawa hatamoto might well have reflected that he was lucky to have a job at all. He may never have needed to exercise the military skills he practised, but the alternative of being a masterless rōnin was not an attractive prospect. Thousands of samurai had been placed in that position after the battle of Sekigahara, which was largely why in 1614 many of them flocked to the standard of Toyotomi Hideyori, the

Three hatamoto in the service of the daimyo of Matsumae relax with a cup or two of *sake*.

son of Hideyoshi, who believed that his rightful inheritance had been stolen by the Tokugawa. When Hideyori's plans came to nothing after the siege of Osaka thousands of rōnin were executed.

Among them was the father of a samurai called Marubashi Chūya. In 1651 the younger Marubashi joined forces with another malcontent called Yui Shōsetsu in a conspiracy to lead rōnin in the overthrow of the Tokugawa government. Both men were employed by the shogunate as martial arts instructors, and thus had access to weapons and extensive contacts with other people who might bear grudges against the Tokugawa. The conspirators' plan was to set fire to Edo on a windy night by letting off an explosion in the gunpowder magazine, and to take over Edo Castle in the resultant confusion. Unfortunately for the plotters, during a bout of delirium Chūya was overheard babbling details of their scheme, and the two ringleaders were arrested and executed. One positive result of this incident, however, was that the government confronted the problem of the rōnin and took steps towards providing employment for them, along with the loyal and long-serving hatamoto who continued to service the machinery of the Tokugawa administration until the dawn of modern Japan.

HORSE GUARDS: ORGANIZATION AND ROLES

As in so many armies throughout the world, the possession and use of horses added a certain status within a circle that was already an elite. Within a lord's hatamoto, mounted troops made up two particular units: the mounted bodyguard or Horse Guards, and the mobile messengers of the Courier Guards.

The first Horse Guards

The earliest use of the expression *uma mawari* ('horse guards') – which is sometimes written with the addition of the honorific prefix '*go*' or '*o*' as 'honourable horse guards' – appears in the '*Taiheiki*', a document concerned

The scene within the *maku* of Hōjō Ujiyasu, as shown on a poor-quality woodblock print; the detail is nonetheless sufficient for us to identify the daimyo Hōjō Ujiyasu surrounded by his hatamoto. At centre, a member of the Courier Guard, displaying a red *sashimono* flag with the *mon* of the Hōjō, kneels in front of his lord.

Okabe Gonnodayū of the Hōjō hatamoto has his *sashimono* flag of a wild boar temporarily removed by an armed servant before going off in search of enemy heads.

with 14th-century warfare. By the Sengoku Period a troop of mounted bodyguards had become the norm, and one of the best-recorded deployments of horse guards at this time is to be found within the ranks of the army of the Hōjō family of Odawara. Five generations of the family, from Hōjō Sōun (1432–1519) to Hōjō Ujinao (1562–91), dominated the Kantō, the plain where modern Tokyo now lies, until they were overcome by Toyotomi Hideyoshi in 1590. A breakdown of the army of the third Odawara Hōjō *daimyo* Ujiyasu (1515–70) for 1559 includes a separate unit of horse guards, listed as 120 guardsmen 'with followers'.

The guardsman was not a simple soldier but a man of consequence, and the 'followers' he supplied were funded from the income derived from the lands he had been granted according to a sliding scale, just like every other retainer in the Hōjō army – although the extra cost of maintaining himself as a horse guardsman was eased by special grants from the daimyo. His followers were samurai, and ashigaru armed variously with spears, arquebuses or bows. Within the historical records there are many examples of the calculation of the military obligations of the wealthier retainers such as guardsmen, listed in ways that make the numbers of followers supplied sound like a fighting platoon with mixed weaponry, but this was not the case in practice. Just as in the example of the late 15th-century European 'lance' led by a knight of moderate means, when they reached the army most of the samurai and footsoldiers supplied according to the muster lists were removed from that officer's direct command, and allocated to assembled samurai units of cavalry and infantry and uniformly-armed ashigaru units. There was also a separate unit of ashigaru who carried flags. For example, Okamoto Masahide of the Hōjō Horse Guards, who was based in Odawara Castle in 1571, was required to supply in addition to his personal service as a mounted guardsman four samurai, six ashigaru spearmen, two ashigaru flag-bearers and four other ashigaru. The samurai, spearmen and flag-bearers would join their fellows in specialist units; it is likely that only the last four ashigaru were retained by Masahide to provide personal services to him, probably as a groom, a weapon-bearer, a 'batman' or orderly, and a porter.

The Yūki regulations

An interesting example of the behaviour expected of the horse guards appears in the family records of the Yūki *kashindan* for 1556. The Yūki were a family established for centuries in Shimōsa province, originally taking their surname from their main castle at Yūki. Yūki Masakatsu (1504–59) was a classic example of a Sengoku daimyo who was constantly at war. He adopted his nephew Yūki Harutomo (1534–1614) as his heir. Harutomo also had no children, and at the suggestion of Hideyoshi he adopted as his heir Hideyasu, the second son of the future shogun Tokugawa Ieyasu, transferring his domains to him in 1590. In the organization of the Yūki retainer band under Masakatsu we find a curious expression for the forces associated with their main castles:

they are referred to by the character '*dō*' that literally translates as 'cave', indicating that these places were the 'lairs' of the Yūki warriors. The Yūki also used the archaic term 'Shitennō' for their four *karō* – Tagaya Shigetsune, Mizutani Shōshun, Yamakawa Shōrin and Iwakami Shinjirō. The first three kept the 'lairs' of Tagaya-dō, Mizutani-dō and Yamakami-dō in the castles of Shimotsuma, Shimodate and Yamakawa respectively, while Iwakami had responsibility for the Yūki-dō that was based in the headquarters castle of Yūki. Each position was hereditary.

The '*Yūki-shi shin-hattō*', the regulations for the domain issued by Yūki Masakatsu in 1556, stretch to a total of 104 articles. This was a time when, just as in the case of the Hōjō, the trend was moving towards organization in warfare rather than a desire for personal glory, and in the following extracts we see an emphasis on fighting in a group:

26. You must not gallop forth as a lone rider, whatever the destination, without receiving orders from the Yūki. But when summoned by the Yūki, you must not be tardy. If you have business that must be attended to or are sick, send a replacement…

67. To gallop forth heedlessly and without thought because you hear the sound of the conch-shell [horn] from the main fort that signals taking to the field is quite unpardonable. If the shell sounds you should go to a village and quickly dispatch some underling or servant to the main fort and have him enquire into where you should go. Only then should you gallop forth…

Two outstanding members of Oda Nobunaga's Horse Guards, Maeda Toshiie and Sassa Narimasa, are shown here in a life-sized diorama at Kiyosu Castle.

Sakai Masanao, a hatamoto of Oda Nobunaga, captured the rice supply being sent by the monks of Mount Hiei to the Asakura army, but while he was waiting for the boat to return he was attacked by samurai from the Asai and Asakura families, and perished.

68. No matter what the emergency, you should not dash off to a battlefield without your armour. Regardless of how brave or prompt you may be, you should not ride out as a lone rider. Wait, form a unit, and only then proceed to the battlefield…

The regulations for the Yūki Horse Guards are even stricter in their insistence upon fighting in a cohesive unit:

72. Men of the Horse Guards should obviously not join an outside group, nor should they join a different group within the Yūki house.

No matter how well they may perform, it will not be acceptable and they will lose face. The Horse Guards should always act in conjunction with ten or twenty other riders and should not mingle with other groups.

Nobunaga's Horse Guards

The best example of the use of horse guards (though also the occasion of their greatest failure) is provided by Oda Nobunaga. Nobunaga's Horse Guards were founded in 1555, and the members of the unit were chosen because of their military skills rather than any impressive family lineage or ancestry. Three future horse guardsmen earned their place in the ranks by their performance at the decisive battle of Okehazama in 1560, an action notable less for the success of Nobunaga's hatamoto than for the failure of the defeated Imagawa Yoshimoto's household troops to protect him.

Having advanced successfully towards Nobunaga's Owari province and captured a castle, Imagawa Yoshimoto rested his troops and prepared to enjoy a traditional head-viewing ceremony within the privacy of his *maku*. It was a stiflingly hot day, and *sake* had been widely distributed among his men, so that when Yoshimoto heard a commotion on the other side of the field-curtains he concluded that a drunken brawl had broken out among his guards. An excited samurai then came running towards him carrying a spear, and Yoshimoto, thinking he was one of his guardsmen, ordered him back to his post. The man turned out to be Nobunaga's hatamoto Hattori Koheita Kazutada (?–1595), who was to earn the distinction of *ichiban yari* ('first into battle') when he aimed his spear at the enemy commander. Yoshimoto grabbed the shaft and made a sword cut at Hattori's leg, but a second samurai named Mōri Shinsuke Yoshikatsu (?–1582) seized him from behind and cut off his head. Both samurai were rewarded for their part in this battle, and continued to serve Nobunaga for many years. Not long afterwards Mōri Yoshikatsu was admitted to the Horse Guards, as was another warrior who distinguished himself at Okehazama by taking three heads. This was Maeda Toshiie (1538–99), who had begun his service to Nobunaga as a page but had suffered disgrace, and was now busy redeeming himself by unofficial participation in Nobunaga's battles. Maeda joined the Horse Guards in 1562 and ended his military career as a daimyo in his own right.

The first Horse Guards were all men from Nobunaga's home province of Owari, and as Nobunaga's career progressed so did their own, as did their numbers. A select few were admitted from conquered territories such as Mino province, which Nobunaga took over in 1567. In 1575 Nobunaga transferred control of Owari and Mino provinces to his son Oda Nobutada and himself took up residence in his magnificent palace-castle of Azuchi. He took many of the Horse Guards with him, although some stayed behind as administrators under Nobutada. In the late 1570s and early 1580s their numbers were further swelled by samurai from the central provinces, but these were always selected on the grounds of military merit.

For the whole of this time and until his death in 1582 the Horse Guards were at Nobunaga's side; for instance,

The former page Maeda Toshiie fought his way back from a period of disgrace by taking part unofficially in Oda Nobunaga's battles. He distinguished himself in this way at the battle of Okehazama in 1560, and was invited to become one of Nobunaga's elite Horse Guards. This statue of him in his later castle town of Kanazawa shows the shape of the red *horo* that distinguished his troop of Horse Guards.

The greatest failure by any unit of guards to protect their master occurred at the Honnōji temple in Kyoto in 1582. Oda Nobunaga, resting overnight on his way to join his army in western Japan, fell victim to a surprise attack by Akechi Mitsuhide. Nobunaga must have had only a few score guardsmen with him, who were completely overwhelmed by men from a rebel army of probably 13,000 men. Here we see Nobunaga (right) defending himself with his sword as arrows pierce the screens.

we read in '*Shinchōko-ki*' for the 16th day of the 10th lunar month (24 November) 1569 that 'the Horse Guards were arrayed and accompanied him to Kyoto'. Elsewhere in the same year they are described as standing guard along with his 'pages, archers and arquebusiers'; but the close relationship between Nobunaga and his Horse Guards is better illustrated by their participation with him in two very unusual events. The first was the bizarre ceremony held to celebrate the New Year in 1574. Nobunaga hosted a banquet where the *sake* flowed freely, but after the guests from 'other provinces' had left a further banquet began for the Horse Guards alone. As more rice-spirit was poured the servants carried into the room the severed heads of Nobunaga's arch-enemies Asakura Yoshikage, Asai Hisamasa and Asai Nagamasa, all taken the previous year. Each head had been carefully coated with gold lacquer, and in front of these prize trophies the exclusive elite of Nobunaga's hatamoto feasted and sang songs.

D. RELIGIOUS IMAGERY, 1590–1615

By the end of the 16th century Japanese body armour had evolved into a strong, practical and fairly plain 'battledress' design, and one way in which a samurai's individual image could be enhanced was to add an elaborate helmet to this standard form of armour. This was popular with daimyo, who had a helmet-bearer to carry it for them and were in any case not expected to fight in it. The elite samurai among a lord's hatamoto were more likely to be distinguished by the wearing of a personally chosen *sashimono* on their backs, either a flag or a three-dimensional creation in lacquered wood and/or paper. These could easily be slipped out of the socket into which they fitted on the back of the armour by an attendant, to allow the wearer to fight freely. Here we see three outstanding examples, each of which has a religious theme. Kinoshita Genzan (**1**), a hatamoto of the Hōjō family of Odawara, is described in the family chronicle '*Hōjō Godaiki*' as wearing a silver *gohei sashimono*; the *gohei* is the device used by Shinto priests to give blessings. Yabe Toranosuke (**2**), who served the Kii branch of the Tokugawa family, set off for the Osaka campaign wearing a *sashimono* in the form of a huge model of an *ihai*, a Buddhist funerary tablet kept in Japanese homes in memory of a deceased relative until being deposited in the family temple. This was chosen, says '*Meiryō Kōhan*', to express Yabe's resolve to die in battle; unfortunately for him he arrived too late to fight, and later starved himself to death in his mortification. Kuruma Tamba-no-kami (**3**) took part in the so-called Tōhoku Sekigahara Campaign in the north in 1600. His name means 'wheel' or 'cart', and he has alluded to this in two ways, as described in '*Aizu-jin Monogatari*'. His *maedate* helmet badge is a golden wheel; but more striking is the image on his *sashimono*, where the cart is being pulled by a demon taking the soul of a female sinner down into Hell.

Less gruesome, but no less telling in its illustration of the closeness of the relationship between Nobunaga and his Horse Guards, is an incident that occurred later in the same year. In Nara may be found the Shōsō-in, the imperial repository where the treasures of Emperor Shōmu (r. AD 724–748) are still preserved. Nobunaga requested that the Shōsō-in should be opened and that he should receive a piece of some very rare fragrant wood kept inside it. The storeroom was opened to the accompaniment of suitable ritual, and pieces of the precious wood were cut off and presented not only to Nobunaga but also to the ten horse guardsmen who were presently in attendance upon him.

It is difficult to determine the total numerical strength of Nobunaga's Horse Guards. In 1568 and again in 1582 we read of 60 guardsmen living in Azuchi Castle while their wives and children stayed at home. His first guardsmen appear to have been 20 in number, and were identified by the wearing of either a black or a red *horo*. A *horo* was a cloak worn on the back, but shaped over a light bamboo framework to give the appearance of a cloth balloon which filled with air as the horseman rode along. The wearing of a *horo* was always regarded as the sign of a distinguished warrior, and if the head was taken from a *horo*-wearer it was customary for it to be wrapped in his *horo* before presentation. Lists of names of the members of the Red and Black Horo Guards vary considerably over the years, but there appear to have been ten men in each unit. A list for 1568 names 19 of the 20, with 16 from Owari, two from Mino, one from Mikawa, and one whose province the author admits that he could not remember. In time these men were to be given considerable personal responsibility when they moved on from service in the Horse Guards. One list of names is as follows:

Red Horo Guards
Maeda Toshiie, Asai Shimpachi, Kinoshita Utanosuke, Itō Kyōzō, Sawaki Yoshiyuki, Iwamuro Nagato-no-kami, Yamaguchi Hida-no-kami, Mōri Nagahide, Iio Hisakiyo, Hasegawa Hashinosuke.

Black Horo Guards
Sassa Narimasa, Kawajiri Hidetaka, Nakagawa Shigemasa, Tsuda Hayato-no-kami, Mōri Yoshikatsu, Hirai Ky'emon, Itō Takebe'e, Mizuno Tatewaki, Matsuoka Kurojirō, Ikoma Katsusuke.

In the '*Shinchōkō-ki*' entry for the 12th day of the 9th lunar month (2 October) 1568 we find a clear statement that Nobunaga's Horse Guards were not limited solely to protection duties. Conducting a campaign against the Rokkaku family, Nobunaga attacked the Rokkaku stronghold of Mitsukuriyama Castle in Omi province. The unusual decision to send his precious guardsmen to lead the attack, instead of other samurai whom a realist would regard as the logical choice for this hazardous role, caused some surprise among his close retainers, and particularly to the 'three men of Mino' (the Sanninshū):

> The previous year [Nobunaga] had brought the large province of Mino under his control. Presumably, thought the men of Mino, on this present occasion he would have them serve as his vanguard; but he did not have such a plan for the Mino-shū, and had his Horse Guards attack Mitsukuriyama [instead]. It was said that the Mino Sanninshū – Inaba Iyo, Ujiie Bokuzen and Andō Iga – expressed admiration for this most unexpected strategy. That night Nobunaga set up his headquarters on Mitsukuriyama...

A composite scene of the greatest hatamoto of the Shimazu family seated around their lord Shimazu Yoshihiro.

The Horse Guards served Nobunaga loyally and well, but by 1582 it had been found necessary for him to appoint five commissioners to take charge of the unit, which they did during the final campaign against Takeda Katsuyori. This implies an increase in the numbers of the guardsmen, and therefore begs the question as to what the Horse Guards were doing during the fateful night that same year at the Honnōji temple, when Nobunaga's life ended.

Several of his leading generals, including Toyotomi Hideyoshi, were fighting the Mōri family in western Japan. Nobunaga was planning to join them, and having left Azuchi Castle he stayed the night en route at the Nichiren temple of Honnōji in Kyoto. There Akechi Mitsuhide (1526–82), another of his generals – who had once been a horse guardsman himself – launched a coup. Mitsuhide's plot had been hatched in such complete secrecy that he only told his four leading captains about it a few hours previously. Their army of 13,000 men had been expecting to march west to attack the Mōri; when they set off in an easterly direction instead it was explained to the men that they were going to be inspected by Nobunaga before leaving for battle, and they were ordered to attack the temple only when they neared the Honnōji compound. The surprise was total and – in an ironic echo of the situation at Okehazama – Nobunaga heard a disturbance outside and thought that a brawl had broken out. His guardsmen, pages and other attendants were completely overwhelmed. Nobunaga committed suicide in the blazing temple, and Akechi's army moved on to another temple where they overcame Nobunaga's heir Nobutada. Quite clearly both

In this detail from a hanging scroll in the museum of the Nikko Tōshogu Shrine we see a number of the senior retainers of Tokugawa Ieyasu who served beneath his flags.

Nobunaga and his son were taken utterly by surprise; the '*Shinchōko-ki*' lists the names of 24 men killed defending him, and although it is impossible to discover whether these were horse guardsmen or pages the small number shows that Nobunaga was surprisingly lightly guarded. The Honnōji incident was the greatest failure of any guards unit to protect their master in the whole of Japanese history.

Hideyoshi's Horse Guards

Nobunaga was avenged by Toyotomi Hideyoshi, who defeated Akechi Mitsuhide and went on to inherit Nobunaga's 'kingdom'. Like his former master, Hideyoshi had his own Horse Guards. When he took over Nagahama Castle in 1573 there appears to have been one unit called the Yellow Horo Guards numbering only seven guardsmen including their followers; by 1581 their number had increased to 18, and Hideyoshi had added two more units, the Red Horo Guards and the Great Horo Guards. The latter name may imply the wearing of an extra-large horo for ceremonial purposes; they were also known as the War Fan Guards, a war fan being an object commonly used in Hideyoshi's army as part of a standard. As an example of one of Hideyoshi's Horse Guards we note the name of Miyata Mitsutsugu, who entered his service in 1573 and was killed during the campaign against Bessho Nagaharu at Miki Castle in 1580.

The Tokugawa Horse Guards

As might be expected, the greatest development in the concept of horse guards is to be found within the ranks of the Tokugawa army. Ieyasu had a mounted bodyguard known as the *Oban* or 'Great Guard' at the time when he took over Edo Castle in 1590. Two years later a considerable reorganization began. The role of the Oban (or *Ogoban* – 'Great Honourable Guard') changed from protecting Ieyasu's person to forming an elite military unit in constant readiness. Five companies were established in 1592; in 1615 the number was raised to ten, with two more being added in 1632. The command structure located the Great Guard under the supervision of one of the *rōjū* (senior councillors) in the Tokugawa *bugyōsho* ('cabinet'). Each company had one *kashira* (captain), four *kumigashira* (lieutenants) and 50 guardsmen. Each company captain had 30 *gokenin* under his personal command, while other guardsmen in the company supplied *gokenin* according to their stipend levels.

The vital role of protecting the future shogun now fell to two other guard units called the Body Guard and the Inner Guard and known collectively as the *Ryōban* ('Two Guards'), whose duties were divided between the castle and the inner palace living quarters. The *Goshoinban* ('Honourable Body Guard') served on night duty within the inner confines of the palace of Edo Castle, and guarded Ieyasu and his successors when they went out. It consisted originally of six companies, later raised to eight, and then to 12 by the addition of the four Nishi-no-maru (Western Bailey) companies for the protection of the heir to the shogunate. These guardsmen wore *horo* of different designs according to their companies. They were commanded by a hatamoto from among the *wakadoshiyori* (junior councillors – a name that otherwise means an 'old head on young shoulders'). Their internal structure was the same as for the Great Guard. In 1606 the *Koshōban* ('Inner Guard') was created, and given responsibility for security within the vast area of Edo Castle that lay outside the palace itself. Six companies covered the main castle and an additional four the Nishi-no-maru. They wore *sashimono* back-flags with slashed edges of seven sections.

In this vignette from the annual re-enactment of the battle of Kawanakajima in Yonezawa, we see details of the flags of Takeda Shingen, including the appropriate centipede motif for his Courier Guards in gold on black.

Finally, in 1643 the first six companies of the *Goshinban* ('Honourable New Guard') were created, two more being added in 1724. The duties of the New Guard consisted of assisting in security within Edo Castle and of providing an advance escort for the shogun when he made visits out of the castle. The structure was similar to that of the other guard units except that each company had 60 guardsmen. They wore very elaborate armour, and used as their *sashimono* a long and impractical *fukinuki* (a streamer such as that used in the Boys' Festival). In all probability the New Guard was only created to accommodate the brothers and relatives of the ladies of the third shogun, Tokugawa Iemitsu, but it certainly provided employment for the younger sons of impoverished hatamoto. One example of a New Guard *sashimono* is shown in Plate H; the accompanying table shows the complete system of identification.

New Guard company	Colours of *fukinuki* (top – middle – bottom bands)
1	Light blue throughout
2	White – dark blue – white
3	White throughout
4	White – red – white
5	Dark blue – white – white
6	Red throughout
Nishi-no-maru 1 (1724)	Dark blue throughout
Nishi-no-maru 2 (1724)	Medium blue throughout

Courier Guards

The other unit within a hatamoto who were mounted as part of their normal duties were the *tsukai-ban* or Courier Guards. They would ride from the *maku* to the generals out on the field, carrying both verbal and written instructions that were too complex to be indicated simply by flags or audible signals. In order to ensure discipline and compliance a command from a Courier Guard was supposed to have the same authority as if it had been personally delivered by the daimyo himself, but we do hear of examples of the

The prominent white flag with the character 'go', seen on this modern painted screen in the museum of the battlefield of Nagakute, identifies a member of Tokugawa Ieyasu's Courier Guards.

recipients arguing with courier guardsmen. For example, during the Winter Campaign of Osaka, Uesugi Kagekatsu had been fighting for a long period, so was ordered to retire by a courier sent from Tokugawa Ieyasu. Kagekatsu was much displeased; he replied that even though the order had come from someone as exalted as the retired shogun, it was not the tradition of the Uesugi to withdraw once a fight had started.

In order to increase their visibility on the battlefield courier guardsmen tended to wear a large *sashimono* flag and often a *horo*, as befitted their status. The flags and *horo* might bear the same devices as those of the guard and line units, but they would always be of a different shape or size so that the Courier Guard stood out. Within the Takeda family the members of the Courier Guard were instantly recognizable by the device of a centipede on their flags. Tokugawa Ieyasu's Courier Guard used the character 'go', the number five – a mystical number associated with the deity Fudo. On some occasions a red *horo* is also noted for the Tokugawa Courier Guard, who during times of war numbered 28. During the Edo Period approximately 40 courier guardsmen served in a special unit.

E **THE HATAMOTO OF TOKUGAWA IEYASU, 1600**
In this plate we reconstruct the founder of the Tokugawa shogunate surrounded by his hatamoto in their original roles 'beneath the flag' at the battle of Sekigahara. Tokugawa Ieyasu (**1**) is seated on his folding camp stool within the privacy afforded by his *maku*, the large field curtains that bear the Tokugawa *mon*. Spread out on a wooden mantlet that acts as a makeshift table is a map of the surrounding area, which is being examined by his *bugyō* (general staff); note too Ieyasu's black-armoured *taisho* Honda Tadakatsu (**2**). Behind Ieyasu squat standard bearers holding the great golden fan that was the most important Tokugawa standard (**3**), and the *ko uma jirushi* of a golden crescent (**4**). Other flag-bearers hold plain white flags, and the banner bearing the motto of the Jōdo sect of Buddhism to which Ieyasu belonged (**5**); it reads 'Renounce this filthy world and attain the Pure Land'. One of Ieyasu's Courier Guards (**6**) has just arrived with important news and kneels before him; he is identified by a *sashimono* bearing the character 'go' (five). His right hand grasps the tip of his sword scabbard, the traditional posture indicating that he has no evil intent towards his master.

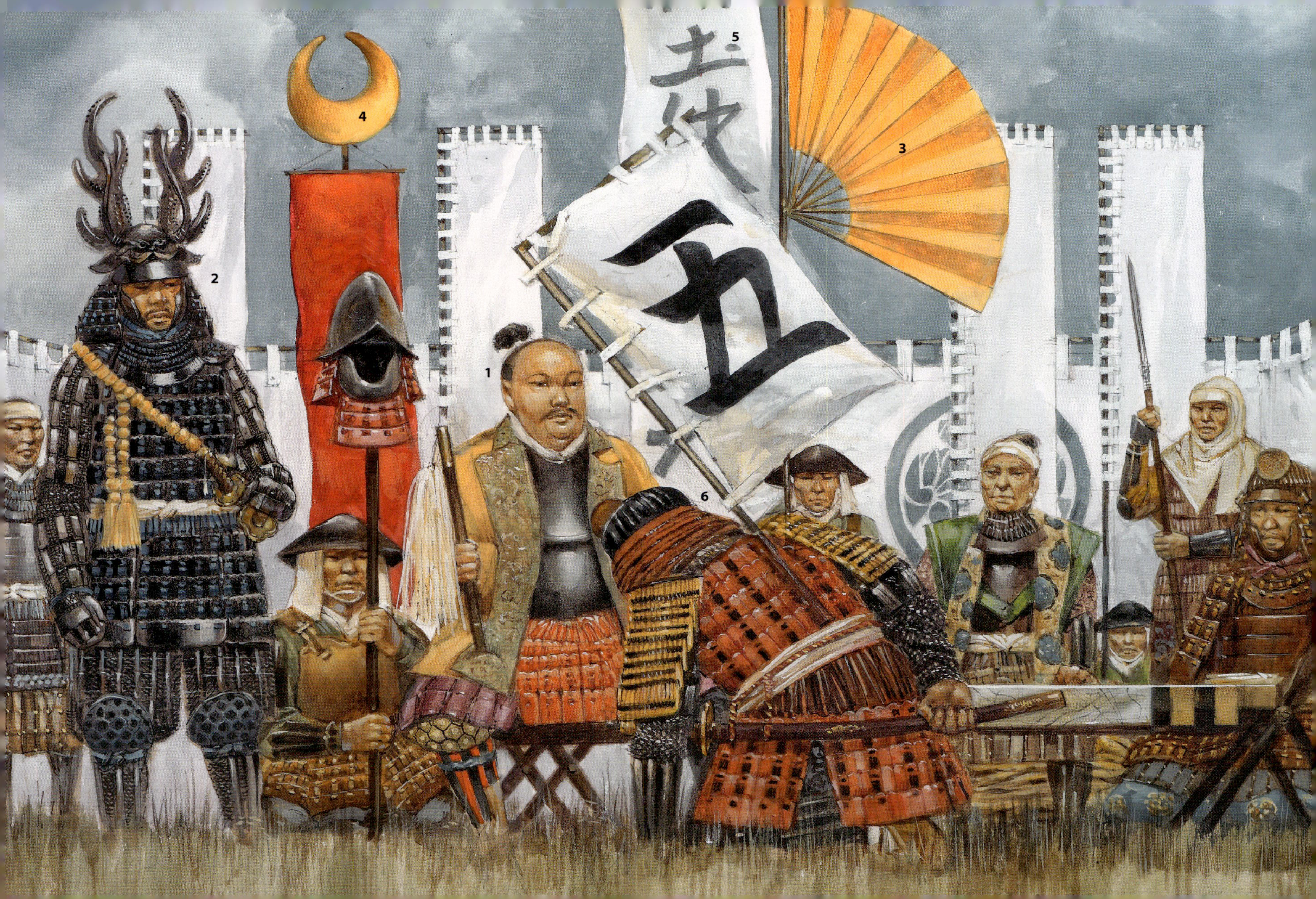
1
2
3
4
5
6

FOOT GUARDS: ORGANIZATION AND ROLES

The Escort Guards

For most of the Sengoku Period no separate word was used that can readily be translated as 'foot guards', even though it is clear from the context that many guardsmen within the hatamoto were not mounted. Instead we simply read of 'guards', with only Horse Guards being singled out as a distinctive unit. It is only with the Edo Period that we come across a named corps of foot guards, and this is within the shogun's own hatamoto; they are known in the literature as the *Kojūninban* (Escort Guards), and are clearly distinguished in the lists from the *Kachi* (footsoldiers). These latter troops, equivalent to the ashigaru of a previous age, were the *yoriki* and the *dōshin* mentioned earlier, who served under the command of officers called *okachi kashira* (captains of footsoldiers) who wore distinctive red *jinbaori* (surcoats), embroidered with various designs based on a device of a fan, to distinguish their units.

The Escort Guards enjoyed a considerably higher status than the other footsoldiers within the shogun's army. Unlike the *okachi kashira*, they belonged to the 'household brigade', although they were themselves regarded as being inferior in rank to the four units of Horse Guards. Their role was to provide a samurai escort on foot in the immediate vicinity of the shogun; this gave them – in common with all bodyguards who had operated on foot throughout the Sengoku Period – an acute and immediate responsibility that the elite Horse Guards could not share. The Escort Guards also provide a rare example of a 'military uniform' among samurai. Ashigaru were commonly issued with identical sets of 'munitions armour' emblazoned with the daimyo's *mon*, but

At the left of this Edo Period marching column, from a wall painting in the museum at the Toshogu Shrine in Nikko, we see members the *Kojūninban* (Escort Guards), the foot guards within the hatamoto of the Tokugawa shogun – see Plate H. They wear identical armour, with their helmets, shoulder-guards and thigh-guards picked out in a contrasting gold lacquer, and leggings striped in blue and white. In front of them march *dōshin* (footsoldiers) carrying spears, bows, and arquebuses in red-lacquered cases.

samurai usually displayed a certain individuality in their costume, the only sign of uniformity within their ranks being by display of the *sashimono*. The shogun's Escort Guards wore identical and distinctive armour, with the *kabuto* (helmet), *sode* (shoulder guards) and *haidate* (thigh guards) all lacquered gold. They also wore blue-and-white striped leggings and a blue-and-white *obi* (belt).

There were initially seven companies of Escort Guards, later raised to 11 with the addition of four Nishi-no-maru companies (see Horse Guards, above). Each was under the command of a *kōjunin kashira* (captain) who had 20 guardsmen under him. The companies were distinguished by means of *sashimono* flags, each one having a differently coloured disc on a differently coloured ground (see Plate H). The colour sequence is given in the accompanying table.

Escort Guard company	Ground colour	Disc colour
1	red	white
2	dark blue	gold
3	white	red
4	dark blue	red
5	halved red and white	dark blue
6	dark blue	white
7	light blue	red
Nishi-no-maru 1	white	dark blue
Nishi-no-maru 2	light blue	gold
Nishi-no-maru 3	red	gold
Nishi-no-maru 4	dark blue	white

The Pages

One expression commonly used for a particular category of hatamoto is *koshō*, a word usually translated as 'page' or 'squire' by analogy with the medieval European equivalents. These men did indeed act as pages during their youth spent within a daimyo's household, and to hold such a position was regarded as a great privilege. Some, such as the future daimyo Katō Kiyomasa (1562–1611), were the sons of dead warriors whose loyalty was repaid by this appointment. When Kiyomasa was orphaned, responsibility for his welfare was taken over by Toyotomi Hideyoshi, who hailed from the same village and had experienced a similarly poor background, and Kiyomasa served Hideyoshi all his life.

Among the most devoted members of a hatamoto were the young *koshō* (pages or squires). Here one holds the sword of the daimyo of Aizu-Wakamatsu, in a life-sized diorama in the Buke Yashiki at Aizu-Wakamatsu.

Other retainers might send their sons as pages to a daimyo as a pledge of their loyalty, or simply so that the boys could receive excellent military training. This would forge a further bond between hatamoto and daimyo; not surprisingly, the personal loyalty shown to a lord by men who had been in his service since boyhood was second to none. Their service in battle placed them adjacent to the daimyo as his 'foot guards' in all but name, and they could be called upon to perform unpleasant tasks without hesitation. One such occasion was when his pages were given the job of executing the numerous prisoners taken when Oda Nobunaga defeated the Ikkō-ikki in Echizen province.

The Colour Guards – communications by flag
The use of flags and standards within a daimyo's army was a highly developed and complex art that went far beyond putting on a brave heraldic display or allowing the identification of a unit or an individual. Both of these functions were, of course, important, and standard-bearers were thus subjected to great personal danger, but an additional reason for the carrying of flags was for the purpose of providing visual signals. Audible signals conveyed by war drums, conch-shell trumpets or gongs had only a limited range, particularly in the din of battle, and the waving of an officer's war fan would only be seen by those in his immediate vicinity. The mounted Courier Guards, although fast and efficient, took time to deliver orders and were vulnerable to enemy atention as they rode about their duties. It therefore fell to a daimyo's *hata bugyō* (flag commissioners) to control a system of communication based on the use of flags.

This appears to have been done using the type of flag known as *nobori*, which was a tall vertical banner threaded onto a pole with a horizontal crosspiece at the top, so that it would not get wrapped around the shaft by the wind and therefore become unrecognizable. We noted above that the troops supplied by Okamoto Masahide of the Hōjō Horse Guards included flag-bearers who would have been allocated to the specialist flag squads, but very little information is available about how these flag squads were actually employed. Sources such as '*Ou Eikei Gunki*' concentrate on individual exploits, as do many of the well-known contemporary painted screens that provide such rich details of Sengoku Period battles. These usually give us a general impression of small-group fighting, but on two particular screens something of the reality of battlefield control is better revealed.

One, owned by Osaka City Museum, is concerned with the Sekigahara campaign, and shows here and there short lines of soldiers – usually no more than eight in number – wearing identical *nobori* on their backs or carrying them in their hands. It is very noticeable that they are intent upon preserving their ranks, and take no part in the fighting going on in front of them. The logical explanation is that the rigorous formation maintained by these flag-bearers has something to do with signalling.

This impression is strengthened by an examination of the painted screen of the battle of Kawanakajima owned by the Nishimura Art Museum in Iwakuni. One side of this screen

Katō Kiyomasa began his military career as a page; when he was orphaned responsibility for his welfare was taken over by Toyotomi Hideyoshi, who came from the same village and had experienced a similarly poverty-stricken childhood. Kiyomasa served Hideyoshi all his life; this statue of him stands in his home village of Nakamura, which now lies within the city of Nagoya.

In the top left-hand corner of this detail from a later painted screen depicting the battle of Nagakute, 1184, may be seen a number of *nobori* vertical banners arranged in a line. These may represent a system for signalling, while the flags seen elsewhere on the screen are personal devices.

depicts a 'slice' or cross-section of the Takeda army, from Takeda Shingen's headquarters forward to his *taishō* Yamagata Masakage in the front line. As all the soldiers are drawn up in ordered ranks the relationships between the various units can be assessed, and it is noticeable that within Yamagata Masakage's division there is a standard-bearer holding one large flag that is the Yamagata *uma-jirushi*, and behind him a line of 20 men each with an identical *nobori*. These would be a means by which signals could be transmitted back to Takeda Shingen in the rear. Shingen's own arrangement of *nobori* is most interesting: he has 30 *nobori*-bearers spread out in front of him but arranged like a letter 'T'. The lower arm of the 'T' faces forwards, and there are ten men in each of the three arms. This arrangement would mean that signalled orders given by Shingen using *nobori* would be visible in all directions.

Records of what these signals were do not appear to have survived, but they are likely to have been specific and uncomplicated commands such as 'attack' or 'withdraw', probably communicated by lowering one section of the *nobori* group while the other was kept vertical, or raising and lowering both. The use of several *nobori* together to create a pattern would be a prominent visual signal, much more noticeable than the waving of a single flag, although we are told that among the Uesugi the flying of a flag bearing the character for a dragon was the signal to attack. Perhaps this basic traditional signal was then augmented or modified using *nobori*?

The use of *nobori* for signalling would be co-ordinated by the *hata bugyō*. On the Kawanakajima screen at Iwakuni several individuals are identified in this role, indicating that they operated in teams of four men, thus making the *hata bugyō* far more of a 'field officer' position than that of a staff officer; this makes the translation as 'colour guards' more meaningful.

Personal attendants

An exclusive body of samurai and ashigaru attended the daimyo himself to provide personal services on a larger scale than those enjoyed by an ordinary samurai. For example, the *zori tori* (sandal-bearer) carried the lord's footwear, amongst other duties equivalent to those of an officer's batman or orderly.

The fierce fighting at the battle of the Anegawa, 1570, showing the flags of the Asakura with white *mon* on red in the upper part. This is a detail from a modern screen painting done in traditional style, and now on display in a museum commemorating the Asai family near Nagahama.

Grooms led his horse, while other ashigaru carried the daimyo's helmet, his spear, his bow, his arquebus or his *naginata* pole-arm. The spear-carrier was regarded as occupying a very honourable role, as was the helmet-bearer, because a daimyo would only place his helmet on his head immediately before the start of a battle; up to that point it would have been carried on a modified spearshaft by a helmet-bearer. The lord's distinctive helmet – often ornamented with horns, feathers, and carved wooden or papier-mâché decorations – was therefore the identifying device closest to the daimyo's person.

Many illustrations show ashigaru in the hatamoto carrying flags, armour boxes, quivers, or an assortment of spears with very elaborate ornamental scabbards. Nor, of course, could a daimyo be expected to carry his own provisions, and an ashigaru would be given the task of carrying his lord's rice in a bag tied at his waist. Other inclusions within the ranks of the hatamoto depended upon the daimyo's personal preferences. Doctors, priests, entertainers, huntsmen, *ninja* and secretaries might all serve 'beneath the flag' as part of his field headquarters entourage. The secretaries *(yūhitsu)* would keep a written log of heads collected, and also compile accounts of the operation, sending written dispatches back and handling all the records required by the daimyo. Ukita Naoie had men in his hatamoto who had charge of his falcons and hunting dogs, while Takeda Shingen employed *sarugaku* (dance drama) performers, along with servants, 884 ashigaru and his Horse Guards.

Many daimyo took along Buddhist priests as 'army chaplains', a function provided in particular by members of the Ji sect of Buddhism. They would perform religious services and could also be counted on to perform funerary *nembutsu*, the ritual of calling on the name of Amida Buddha. They might even advance during the midst of battle – at great risk to their own lives – to offer *nembutsu* to the spirits of those who had just fallen. They also provided memorial services, and would perform the useful act of visiting relatives of the slain and reporting deeds back to the home temple, as in the following account:

> Monks and priests who were relatives collected the remains and embraced the dead bodies. They grieved and wept without limit. Such a thing has

never been heard of in the past nor seen in our own time. Those *jishū* gathered up one by one the corpses lying scattered here and there. Some they burnt and others they buried. They set up *stupas* and on each they bestowed *nembutsu*. Everywhere they raised the hope that Amida would come to lead them to paradise. More and more they acted with the mercy of Buddha. They went so far as to collect [the last] writings from the dead as souvenirs which were sent to the widows and orphans.

HATAMOTO IN ACTION

Breaching the *maku*

The battles of Kawanakajima in 1561 and Imayama in 1570 provide two examples of the defences of a *maku* being breached, but with contrasting results. At Kawanakajima the hatamoto succeeded in beating off the attack, while at Imayama the results were similar to the disaster at Okehazama.

The battle of Kawanakajima in 1561 was the fourth out of five battles to be fought in roughly the same location between the armies of Takeda Shingen (1521–73) and Uesugi Kenshin (1530–78). The battle came about as a result of clever moves and counter-moves conducted by these rival generals under the cover of darkness. The Uesugi army had taken up positions on the hill of Saijoyama, from where they threatened Takeda Shingen's forward position of Kaizu Castle. Shingen's plan was to deploy his army in secrecy across the river from Kaizu; a detachment would then launch a surprise attack on the Saijoyama position from the rear and drive the Uesugi down against the waiting ranks of the main Takeda army. However, Uesugi Kenshin anticipated the move, and instead launched a surprise dawn attack himself on the Takeda position.

When the attack came Takeda Shingen was seated within the curtains of the *maku*, and probably had no physical defences other than the possible use of the wooden mantlet shields employed by ashigaru missile troops. Everything

Seated on his camp stool, Uesugi Kenshin (right, in monk's cowl) receives the homage of his hatamoto in the annual pageant in Yonezawa depicting the Uesugi army's departure for war. This colourful festival takes place on the evening before the annual re-enactment of the battle of Kawanakajima.

depended on the human shield of the hatamoto. According to the 'Kōyō Gunkan', the surprise attack that came out of the dawn against the Takeda was aimed directly at the field headquarters, and was even led by the opposing commander Uesugi Kenshin himself. This account relates that the attack came close to killing Takeda Shingen in spite of his 20-man personal bodyguard and 18 pages:

> Just then a warrior wearing a pale green *haori* [sleeveless jacket], with his head wrapped in a monk's white cowl, riding a cream-coloured horse and holding a three-*shaku* [1m-long] sword, charged right up to Lord Shingen, who was sitting on his camp stool. He aimed at him three times with his sword, and only just missed him each time. Shingen took the blows on his war fan, which was discovered to have eight cuts on it when it was later examined. His *karō* and his 20-man bodyguard unit, each of whom was a brave warrior, fought back furiously, making a wall around him in case he should be seen by friend or foe and cutting down anyone who came close. The *karō* Hara Osumi-no-kami took hold of Shingen's spear, which was inlaid with mother-of-pearl, and thrust it at the warrior in the green coat on the cream-coloured horse, but he missed his target. He aimed at the top of the warrior's armour but instead only caught the horse's rump; at this the horse reared and bolted.

Uesugi Kenshin's remarkable attack was beaten off, but the outcome of a similar incident that took place at Imayama in 1570 was different. In this latter action the army of the Otomo clan under Otomo Chikasada were besieging Saga Castle, the seat of the daimyo Ryūzōji Takanobu (1530–85). Their large army was spread out in a semicircle around Saga, and so confident were they of victory that Otomo Chikasada organized a celebration within his *maku* in anticipation. When news of this reached the Saga garrison, it seemed to Nabeshima Naoshige (1537–1619), one of Ryūzōji's hatamoto (and a man who one day would become a daimyo in his own right) that the opportunity was perfect for a night sortie.

The raiding party moved into action in complete darkness and opened fire with arquebuses as they neared the *maku*. The samurai charged in, kicking over the iron braziers in which logs burned to provide the only

F · MUKAI TADAKATSU SAILS TO OSAKA, 1614

As the *fune bugyō* (commissioner of ships, admiral) to the first and second Tokugawa shoguns, Mukai Shogen Tadakatsu (1582–1641) held a key position within the Tokugawa hatamoto and, having been created a daimyo in his own right, he also had his own corps of close retainers including guards, messengers and standard-bearers, all of whom we see represented here. The Mukai family originally hailed from Ise province. Mukai Masatsuna (1557–1610) had served Takeda Katsuyori, but joined Tokugawa Ieyasu when the latter defeated the Takeda in 1582, the year when Masatsuna's son Tadakatsu was born. For his service against the Hōjō during the Odawara campaign of 1590 Masatsuna received a grant of land from the future shogun and the appointment of *fune bugyō*. Here we see his son Tadakatsu (**1**), who inherited the post, sailing for Osaka Castle in 1614 to support the Tokugawa siege with the warships and supply vessels under his command. Wearing his personal *sashimono* with the character 'mu' written in *hiragana* script, Tadakatsu is attended by three standard-bearers. His 'great standard' (**2**) is a large golden bell topped with a plume of red-dyed yak hair; a similar plume appears above his 'first lesser standard' (**3**) which consists of five golden lanterns, while an additional standard (**4**) is a silver swastika, an ancient Buddhist symbol. His Courier Guard (**5**) has a black-and-white *horo* with a slashed golden flag. The foot guards in attendance upon him (**6**) wear a white *sashimono* with a red sun disc; the ashigaru in his hatamoto (**7**) have flags with five red suns on white.

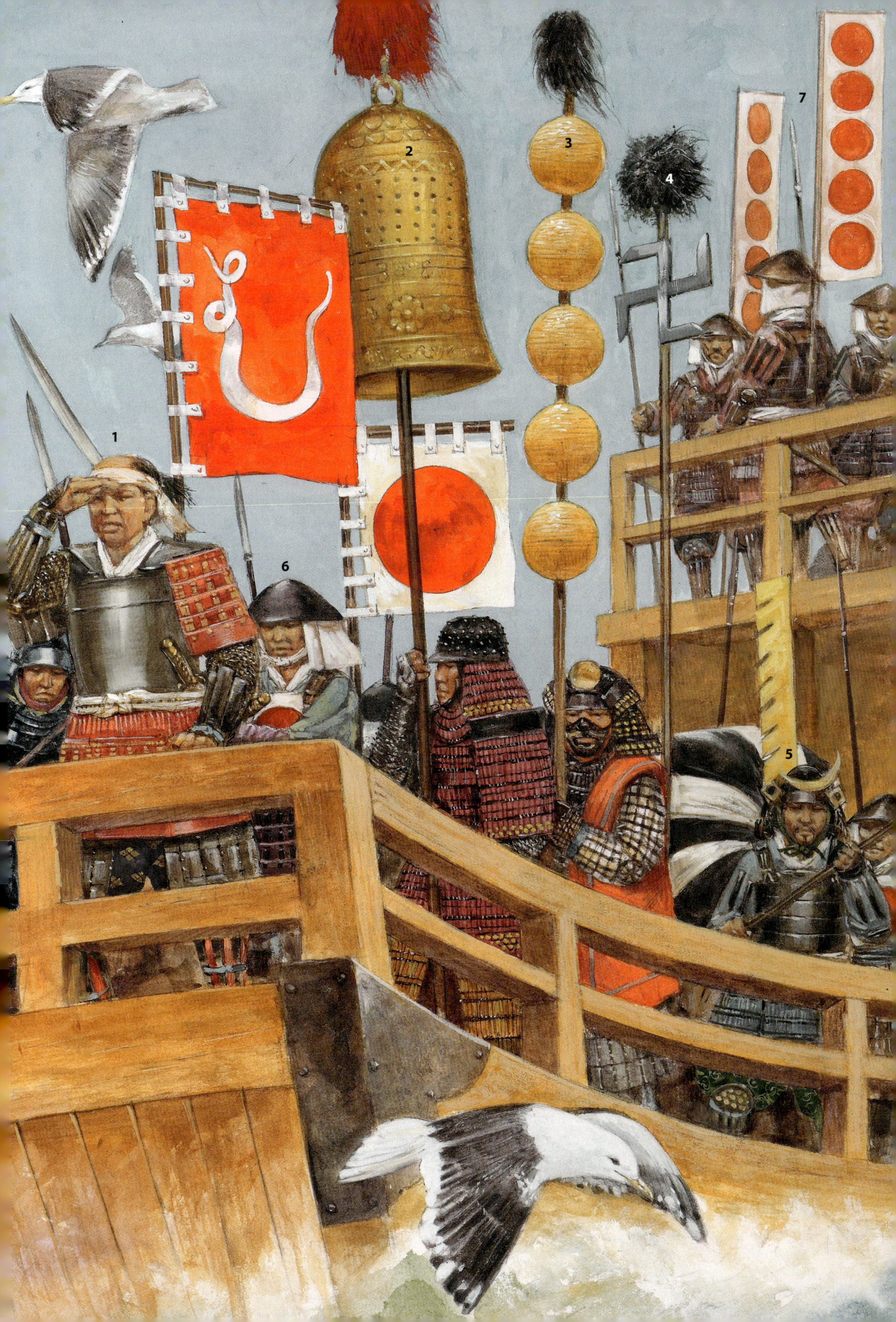
1
2
3
4
5
6
7

'Devil' Kojima Yatarō was a hatamoto of Uesugi Kenshin. He is depicted here with a severed head in his hand, and a grinning *oni* (demon) on his *sashimono*. Note the brackets and cord detail.

illumination, and the result was a massacre; Otomo Chikasada was killed, and a high proportion of his hatamoto were cut down within the *maku* that it was their duty to protect.

THE NORTHERN HATAMOTO, 1591–1603

The Onodera and the Mogami

One of the great natural frontiers of pre-modern Japan lay along the summit of the huge bulk of Mount Chōkai in Tōhoku in the far north-east. This was within the ancient province of Dewa, and is today the border between

Yamagata and Akita prefectures. In the late Sengoku Period it marked the interface between the territory of the Onodera family, who ruled most of what is now the southern part of Akita, and their rivals the Mogami to the south. Almost three decades of warfare took place as the Onodera established their own pre-eminent position against minor clans in the locality, and then faced invasions by the Mogami. In 1600, however, they were all caught up in what is commonly referred to as the Tōhoku Sekigahara campaign, a bitter struggle between supporters of Tokugawa Ieyasu and their local rivals. In the accounts of the fighting in this part of Japan, recorded mainly in '*Ou Eikei Gunki*', we find many instances of bravery on the battlefield by hatamoto – and of an even more remarkable resilience off it, as survivors from their daimyo's bands of retainers fought on even though their cause was hopeless.

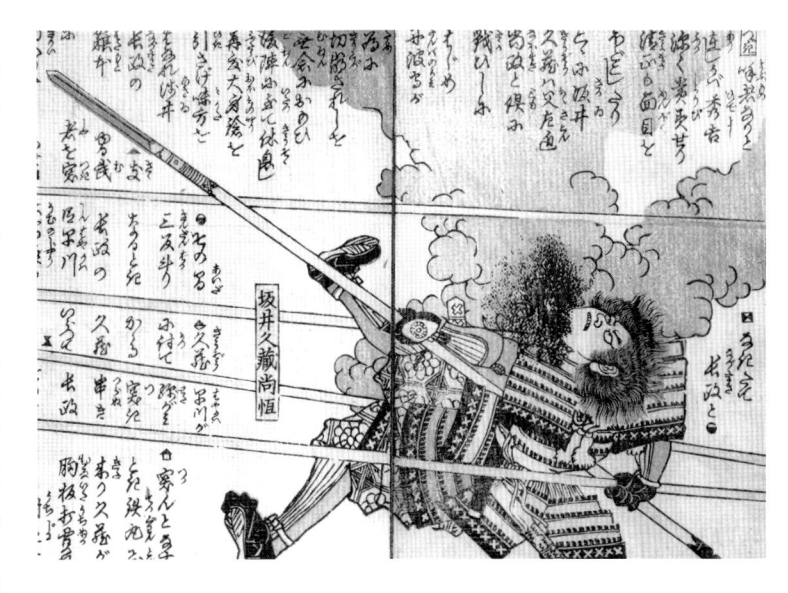

Sakai Narishige, the son of Sakai Masanao, mounted a one-man attack on the *maku* of Asai Nagamasa at the battle of the Anegawa, 1570. He was unhorsed by the vigilant Asai hatamoto, and then shot dead when over a hundred arquebusiers in the guard opened fire on him.

In common with most of the other Sengoku Period daimyo who enjoyed a personal hegemony before they were overcome by the massive armies assembled by leaders such as Oda Nobunaga and Toyotomi Hideyoshi, the Onodera controlled a large number of mountaintop castles, some of which were little more than guard posts. Most of these forts were built along the line of the mighty Omonogawa river, which flows north from Mount Chōkai and acted as a protective moat for the Onodera's headquarters castle of Yokote, from where the current daimyo Onodera Yoshimichi ruled his domain. His younger brother Yasumichi was stationed in Omori, while his illegitimate older brother Shigemichi was the keeper of Nishimonai. The other castles were under the control of loyal hatamoto. Two different approaches to listing the Onodera retainer band have been preserved in the family records. The first lists the 'civil' officers of the hatamoto as:

Tairō (senior minister or *karō*)	1
Wakadoshiyori (junior councillor)	1
Bugyō	3
Senior retainers 'without portfolio'	43
Satellite castle wardens	14

The '*Ou Eikei Gunki*' records the Onodera army as follows; the expression *ki* is the counting suffix for mounted samurai, not for individuals but including the men supplied by that individual warrior, so is roughly equivalent to the medieval European 'lance':

Hatamoto, *yoriki* and *baishin* (a samurai's own retainers)	1,300 *ki*
Other horsemen	300 *ki*
Farmer-samurai	100 *ki*
Ashigaru	2,300-plus

All the fighting between the Onodera and the Mogami was to be carried out against a background of major events occurring elsewhere in Japan, but sometimes with so little regard for them that these northern daimyo appeared to be living in a world of their own. The first time that such wider affairs impinged upon their local rivalries was in 1591, when a rebellion at Kunohe Castle in neighbouring Mutsu province prompted an intervention by Toyotomi Hideyoshi, whose defeat of the Hōjō at Odawara in 1590 had been a major step forwards in his programme of reunification. Many of the northern daimyo, such as the great Date Masamune (1566–1636), had then pledged allegiance to Hideyoshi, and Hideyoshi's general Gamō Ujisato was entrusted with the task of bringing the remaining northern lords to heel. When Kunohe Masazane was killed defending Kunohe Castle, Japan was officially reunified.

From 1592 onwards Toyotomi Hideyoshi was preoccupied with his planned conquest of China, a disastrous expedition that got no further than Korea and inflicted great damage on that unfortunate country. These overseas distractions were probably the main reason why fighting was able to continue between rival daimyo in remote Dewa province even after they had all supposedly pledged a common allegiance to the new central power.

As a result, while many of the daimyo from other parts of Japan were fighting on the Korean peninsula in 1593, the Onodera were facing an invasion of their own from their major rivals the Mogami, who were led for the whole of this time by their daimyo Mogami Yoshiaki (1546–1614) from his castle of Yamagata. He probably had Hideyoshi's blessing to bring the stubborn Onodera under control, yet to Mogami Yoshiaki it was no more than a further stage in the families' ongoing hostilities.

Mogami Yoshiaki's primary objective was Ono Castle, one of the Onodera fortresses nearest to the border, which was hastily reinforced by part-time farmer-samurai. According to the '*Ou Eikei Gunki*', the Mogami could see from across the Omonogawa river that the castle was packed with samurai. Their

The Fourth Battle of Kawanakajima saw active participation in the fighting by the rival commanders Takeda Shingen and Uesugi Kenshin. Here Uesugi Kenshin, wearing a monk's white cowl and a green *haori* and riding a pale horse, engages Takeda Shingen in personal combat. Curiously, the artist for this modern reprint of '*Ehon Koetsu Gunki*' – a work dealing with the fighting between the Takeda and the Uesugi – has chosen to show the famous action taking place in the middle of a river rather than within the Takeda *maku*, as related in some accounts of the battle.

first attack across the river was heavily defeated, so they waited until the break of dawn before trying again, making a successful river crossing while using wooden shields to protect them from arquebus fire. The attack was pressed home and the Onodera troops fled, pausing only to throw away at the riverside the heads they had taken the night before. Ono Castle was then burned to the ground.

The Mogami advance was not to be undertaken by military means alone, and in 1594 Mogami Yoshiaki spread false rumours that the *karō* of the Onodera, Hachikashiwa Michinari, was planning to betray his master. Onodera Yoshimichi did not wait for proof to be found but had his man assassinated, thus severely damaging the unity that was so vital among the hatamoto. A year later Mogami Yoshiaki took advantage of the situation he had created and invaded the Onodera territories once again. This time his target was the castle of Yuzawa, held by the brothers Onodera Magoshichirō and Magosaku. Yuzawa lay on the flat plain to the north of Mount Chōkai, and its position just to the south of a tributary of the Omonogawa made it Yokote Castle's most important satellite defensive position. When Yuzawa fell:

> The castellan Magoshichirō first of all killed his wife and children, the retainers stabbed to death their wives and children as a sacrifice, [then] they set fire to the castle and again fought fiercely, killing in the enemy's midst. Ultimately they threw off their helmets and committed *seppuku*.

In 1596 the Mogami army once again surprised their enemies, by unexpectedly crossing one of the mountain passes in deep snow, and met the Onodera samurai in battle at Oshimabara:

> The battlefield was a scene of carnage for any friend or foe who entered it to fight there. A samurai appeared who had taken an enemy general's head. Spears and *naginata* were wielded freely, and in one brief moment 18 men from the *nagae-yari* [long-spear squad] on the Yokote side [i.e. the Onodera] brought down more than 30 men, while Takada Ubasuke thrust [his spear] through the body of a hatamoto of the Mogami over the top of his armour…

Omori Castle

One by one the smaller Onodera fortresses surrendered to the Mogami, and it looked as though Onodera rule might well collapse entirely within a few years. Moreover, the Onondera were soon faced with yet another setback and a new enemy. While the war in Korea was still continuing, Toyotomi Hideyoshi ordered a major land survey of Japan. One result in Tōhoku was

Yamanaka Shikanosuke provides an excellent example of a loyal *hatamoto*. In this statue on the site of the castle of Toda we see him making a vow to the three-day old moon that he would restore the fortunes of the Amako family.

The great daimyo Date Masamune, shown here beside his castle in Sendai, took a prominent role in the early stages of the Tōhoku Sekigahara campaign; otherwise the campaign was largely fought by hatamoto from the rival sides. Masamune is shown with his characteristic crescent-moon *maedate* (helmet crest).

that the Onodera fief was reduced in size, and part of it, including Yuzawa Castle, was given to their hated enemies the Mogami. As if this was not humiliation enough, the Onodera acquired a new adversary in the person of Otani Yoshitsugu (1559–1600), whom Hideyoshi had entrusted with ensuring that the new arrangements were complied with, that the survey was up to date and that taxes were collected. The Onodera resisted this imposition as fiercely as they had withstood the Mogami invasions.

Thus it was that in the winter of 1599–1600 Onodera Yasumichi was faced with an attack by Otani Yoshitsugu against the fortress of Omori, a naturally strong position built at the confluence of two rivers. Local resentment over the boundary revisions had been considerable at all social levels, so it was a heterogeneous garrison of Onodera hatamoto, samurai and farmers that defended Omori against the Otani army. In the '*Ou Eikei Gunki*' we have excellent references to a *maku* and to the Otani hatamoto:

> The inhabitants of the vicinity carried food supplies into the castle, and over 300 people crammed into the San-no-maru [third bailey]. On the 18th day of the same month an attack began from three sides, and the commander Yasumichi led a sally out with 300 men, going forward two *ri* [*c.* 8km, or 5 miles] and bursting into the *maku* that bore the *mon* of a bird's feathers, but he held back when he saw the towering flags fluttering splendidly in the mountain breeze… Nikaho, in command of the second guards unit, was caught in the fighting and the hatamoto who fought beside the general were broken and pulled back. A certain Madarame was fighting his first campaign at the age of 14, but he was met by the spears of the enemy and died.

The fighting continued the following day, in the bitter cold of a Tōhoku winter:

> …rain fell continually, washing their armour as the wind blew, forcefully hitting the faces of men and horses, so that their hands froze both

G **HATAMOTO ON THE KANTŌ, 1540–1614**

The Kantō plain, the fertile area of eastern Japan where Metropolitan Tokyo and Yokohama now lie, belonged to the Hōjō family for much of the 16th century, but passed to Tokugawa Ieyasu when the Hōjō were defeated at Odawara in 1590. Here we see representatives of the Horse Guards and Courier Guards of both these families. In Hōjō service is Okabe Gonnodayū (**1**), who, according to the '*Hōjō Godaiki*', temporarily discarded his unwieldy *sashimono* with its depiction of a wild boar when he went off in search of enemy heads. However, the abandoned flag was taken by an enemy samurai who wore it on his own back, and then gave it back to Okabe in return for the severed head of his comrade. Matsu Hidenobu (**2**) wears a *horo* of white feathers behind an antler *sashimono*, and wields a large rake (*ō-kumade*). At Sekigahara he used it to drag down 11 men, who were then beheaded by his retainers. Okubo Shichiro'emon Tadayo (1531–93) from the Tokugawa hatamoto (**3**), whose use of a three-dimensional golden butterfly is recorded in the '*Kōyō Gunkan*', appears on the painted screen of the battle of the Anegawa owned by Fukui Prefectural Museum.

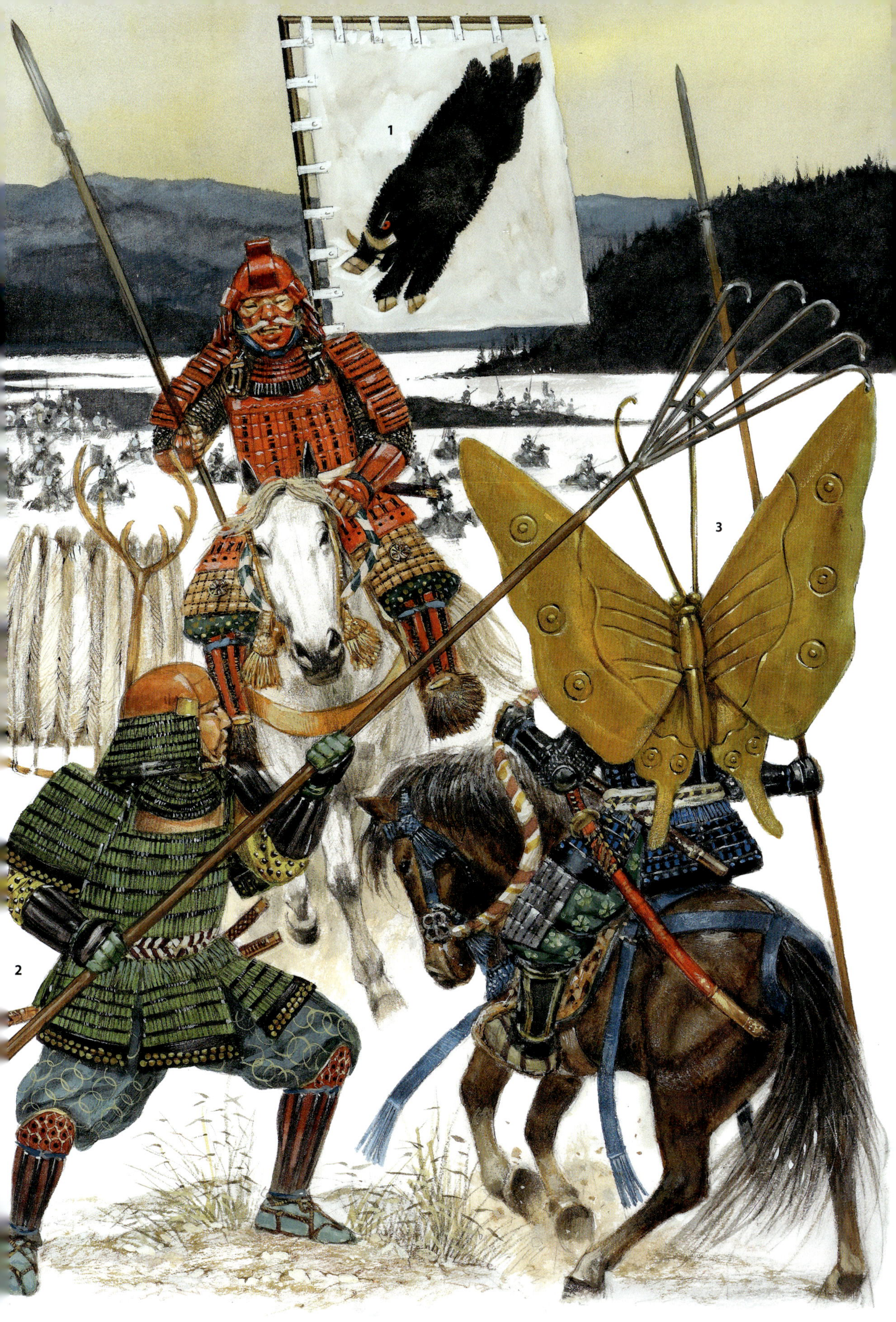
1
2
3

as they drew their bows and also when firing arquebuses, of which the match-cords were immediately extinguished, and they became exhausted. But the Omori force had kindled a fire in the administrative headquarters building in the middle of the stockade, so they warmed their hands and feet on the burning charcoal, and then rode out by turns, tilting their bamboo hats and striking at the arquebuses, taking every opportunity to loose arrows and mount an attack.

Even a surprise attack at the rear of the fortress – which the author of the account likens to Minamoto Yoshitsune's famous descent of a cliff at the battle of Ichinotani in 1184 – failed to make any impression on the defenders, who further demonstrated their solidarity when women in the garrison used catapults to shoot stones down onto the Otani samurai:

> About twenty arquebuses opened fire. This was not enough to frighten [the women], and the hurling of small stones from the shadows of the moat was like a hailstorm. To the irritation of Shiyoshi, they struck Ishii Ukon Koremichi in both eyes and killed him. Similarly, they struck in one eye the horse that Kutsuzawa Goro was riding with his bow hand, but did not kill it. Saying, 'to stay too long in that place and be hit by women's stones would be a failure bringing ridicule for generations to come', they returned to the starting point of their attack.

This equestrian statue of Mogami Yoshiaki stands inside the courtyard of his castle of Yamagata. Mogami was the deadly enemy of the Onodera and conducted several campaigns against them, until both families were caught up in the turmoil following Toyotomi Hideyoshi's death.

This unsuccessful siege of Omori Castle exhausted Otani Yoshitsugu, who was already suffering from the advanced stages of leprosy, and he abandoned his attempt to manage the rebellious northerners. Toyotomi Hideyoshi, who had given him the task, was now dead, and had left behind a five-year-old son, Hideyori, as his heir. Yoshitsugu turned his mind towards deciding where his loyalties might lie as all the daimyo began to line up for the coming struggle over Hideyori's inheritance. Otani Yoshitsugu threw in his lot with the pro-Toyotomi Hideyori coalition, and October of 1600 was to see him fighting for Ishida Mitsunari against Tokugawa Ieyasu on the losing side at the battle of Sekigahara. His leprosy was now so bad that he had to be carried onto the battlefield in a palanquin from which he directed his troops, while confined within his *maku*. When he realized that the battle was lost he committed suicide.

Mogami Yoshiaki, the old enemy of the Onodera, chose the Tokugawa side, and after his service in the Tōhoku Sekigahara campaign (as described below) he was richly rewarded.

Yoshiaki's new position under Tokugawa Ieyasu finally allowed him to settle his old scores with the Onodera; his great rival Onodera Yoshimichi was stubborn to the last, and in spite of what he had suffered at the hands of Hideyoshi's representative Otani Yoshitsugu he had perversely become the only daimyo in the Akita area to embrace the pro-Hideyori cause. The loss of all his allies after Sekigahara left Onodera Yoshimichi precariously isolated, so in the winter of 1600–01 Mogami Yoshiaki sent an army against him.

The three castles of Yokote, Omori and Nishimonai commanded by the three Onodera brothers were now like small boats in a huge sea. Yoshiaki's first objective was Onodera Yasumichi's castle of Omori, the place that had resisted an attack so well only a year previously. Yasumichi ordered that the town around the castle should be burned down, and 800 farmer-samurai entered the castle as part of a scorched-earth policy to deny shelter and supplies to the enemy. But the political tide had now turned so drastically that the Onodera had little support beyond their own family, and Mogami Yoshiaki won a comparatively easy victory. Onodera Yasumichi took a considerable personal role in the fighting, carrying a large *naginata*, but in the middle of a fierce blizzard the castle fell and Yasumichi was captured.

The fall of Omori turned out to be the last battle of the Onodera. Realizing that further resistance was useless, the daimyo Onodera Yoshimichi surrendered Yokote Castle and accepted whatever fate Tokugawa Ieyasu should decide for him. His punishment was to be exile to the castle town of Tsuwano, a place located almost at the furthest point of the main Japanese island of Honshū and as far away from Akita as it was possible to go without crossing the sea. There, in 1601, he was placed under the care of the local daimyo; he was later joined by his brother Yasumichi, and lived to the age of 80, dying in the year 1645.

Despite the fall of Onodera Yoshimichi, at the last surviving Onodera stronghold – the fortress of Nishimonai, held by Yoshimichi's illegitimate elder brother Shigemichi – an extraordinary episode was about to begin. Two months after the exile of Yoshimichi, the Mogami general Sakenobe Norikatsu came to take possession of Nishimonai, but was met by armed

Otani Yoshitsugu acted as Hideyoshi's land surveyor and tax collector in remote Dewa province, where he failed to capture the Onodera fortress of Omori. Suffering badly from leprosy, he took part in the battle of Sekigahara, 1600, from a palanquin placed within his *maku*. Here he is depicted preparing for death at his own hand after the defeat; his *mon* is dark blue on the white curtains, and the banners show three white discs.

The daimyo Shima Sakon is shown here at Sekigahara wearing a gold *fukinuki* as a *sashimono*, and followed by a standard-bearer carrying his personal banner. This is a detail from a painted screen in the museum of Sekigahara Warland.

resistance. Sixty Mogami samurai were killed by the Onodera hatamoto, after which the aged Onodera Shigemichi set fire to the castle and, according to some accounts, perished in the flames. The surviving hatamoto then did an unusual thing in his memory; they danced. It had long been the local tradition to perform a dance in the temple ground to pray for a good harvest, so in 1601 the dance was performed as a way of marking the passing of the last commander of Nishimonai Castle. This dance is still performed today in Nishimonai town to mark the festival of Bon, when the spirits of the ancestors revisit the places where they lived.

Last defiance of the Onodera hatamoto

The Onodera fief now no longer existed, and apart from the handful of followers who had been allowed to accompany Yoshimichi into exile at Tsuwano his loyal hatamoto were now all rōnin, whose future was to be determined by the massive convulsions in the social structure of Japan that the new shogun, Tokugawa Ieyasu, instigated in 1603. Under this drastic scheme all the daimyo – whether they had been *fudai* or *tozama* – were subject to a major redistribution of territory according to a plan of relocation whereby the trusted *fudai* could keep an eye on the suspect *tozama*. Few daimyo were allowed to retain possession of their ancestral lands. The rich province of Hitachi, for example, was taken from the *tozama* daimyo Satake Yoshinobu and given to Tokugawa Yorifusa, Ieyasu's ninth son, while Satake Yoshinobu was sent to Tōhoku and given the old Onodera territory.

In virtually all cases throughout Japan this transition, whereby a daimyo family that might have been in the locality for centuries was uprooted in favour of another who had been similarly wrenched from his own ancestral territory, was a comparatively peaceful process – but not in Akita.

The Onodera lord had not been moved to another territory, but had been exiled as a political prisoner, and there was great local resentment. Yokote Castle was still a smouldering ruin, so the incoming Satake Yoshinobu established himself temporarily in the minor fortress of Rokugo. There, in the tenth lunar month of 1603, he was to find himself besieged by 1,000 surviving retainers of the Onodera in a final suicidal gesture. The rebellion was soon overcome, but no hatamoto in Japanese history were ever to express their loyalty to their distant lord in such a dramatic fashion.

WAR BY DELEGATION

The Tōhoku Sekigahara campaign, 1600

The story of how Mogami Yoshiaki, who took no part in the battle of Sekigahara, instead rendered equally valuable service to Tokugawa Ieyasu in the north-west provides a case study of how the command of armies could be delegated to trusted hatamoto. Of the three daimyo who were involved in this vital campaign – which could easily have reversed the outcome of Sekigahara – one, Date Masamune, played an active role only in the initial stages, but his ally Mogami Yoshiaki was fully involved throughout. Their rival, the anti-Tokugawa lord Uesugi Kagekatsu (1555–1623) from Aizu-Wakamatsu Castle, delegated the entire conduct of the campaign to his trusted hatamoto, in particular to Naoe Kanetsugu (1560–1620), a brilliant general who achieved a remarkable co-ordination of separate forces on his master's behalf.

Mogami Yoshiaki's decision to support the Tokugawa reflected the fact that he had no great love for the late Toyotomi Hideyoshi and his family. His daughter had been married to Hideyoshi's nephew Hidetsugu, the man who had been Hideyoshi's original choice as his heir, but when his son Hideyori was born Hideyoshi changed his mind. The thwarted Hidetsugu reacted most unwisely and, accused of treason, he was exiled to the monastery of Koyasan. There, in 1595, he was ordered to commit suicide, and the following month his wife, daughters and ladies-in-waiting (84 women in all) were beheaded. It is therefore little wonder that when Hideyoshi died in 1598 and the daimyo were called upon to declare their loyalty, Mogami Yoshiaki sided with Tokugawa Ieyasu rather than the nominal supporters of the heir Hideyori, whose cause had cost his daughter's life.

After some preliminary moves by Data Masamune, Uesugi Kagekatsu took the

When Onodera Shigemichi was defeated and died at Nishimonai Castle in 1601 his surviving hatamoto performed a traditional local dance in his honour. This is now performed every year in Nishimonai, at the time of the Bon festival when the spirits of the dead are welcomed back into the village. This statue shows the costumes worn by the types of dancers.

In this detail from the painted screen depicting the battle of Hasedo in the Mogami Historical Museum in Yamagata we see the *hatamoto* Tsunashima Shōheimon, who fought under the flag of an axe. This flag is carried on the back of his retainer, while Tsunashima waves his war fan.

initiative in the campaign in the person of his hatamoto Naoe Kanetsugu, who was based in the castle of Yonezawa. His objective was Mogami Yoshiaki's castle of Yamagata, and Kanetsugu skilfully organized three separate armies to move against it. His main body of 20,000 men circled round to approach from the west, while his second division of 4,000 men under Hommura Chikamori headed straight north towards Yamagata, a move that brought them first against the castle of Kaminoyama to the south of Yamagata, held by Satomi Minbu. Meanwhile a third division of 3,000 led by Shima Yoshitada advanced via Shonai to the north of Yamagata.

Naoe Kanetsugu's main body encountered their first obstacle in Hataya Castle, defended by the redoubtable Eguchi Gohei. As soon as word was brought to him of the advance of Kanetsugu's army he gave orders for the

H. HORSE AND FOOT GUARDS OF THE SHOGUN TOKUGAWA IEMITSU, 1643

The *Kojūnin* (Escort Guards) were the foot guards to the shoguns, but enjoyed a markedly lower social status than the Horse Guards; here we reconstruct guardsmen in the service of the third Tokugawa shogun. The Escort Guardsman (**1**) belongs to the Fifth Company, as shown by the design of his *sashimono*. His armour is of a simple standardized form, although it is set off by the blue-and-white leggings he is wearing. The mounted guardsman, who is sporting a black polka-dot *horo* (**2**), is from the *Shōin Ban* (Body Guard), and belongs to the Second Company of the Nishi-no-maru (Western Bailey) of Edo Castle. The main units of the Body Guard had responsibility for protecting the person of the shogun, while the Nishi-no-maru troops watched over his heir. Nevertheless, both these warriors are overshadowed in magnificence by the representative from the Second Company of the *Shinban* (New Guard), who guarded nothing in particular but always looked dazzling (**3**). The New Guard, formed in 1643, may well have been created to find employment for the numerous progeny of the Shogun Iemitsu. This guardsman wears a fine suit of gold-lacquered armour with a curved shell helmet-badge; his *sashimono* is a long and impractical *fukinuki*, the streamers commonly seen in the Boys' Festival.

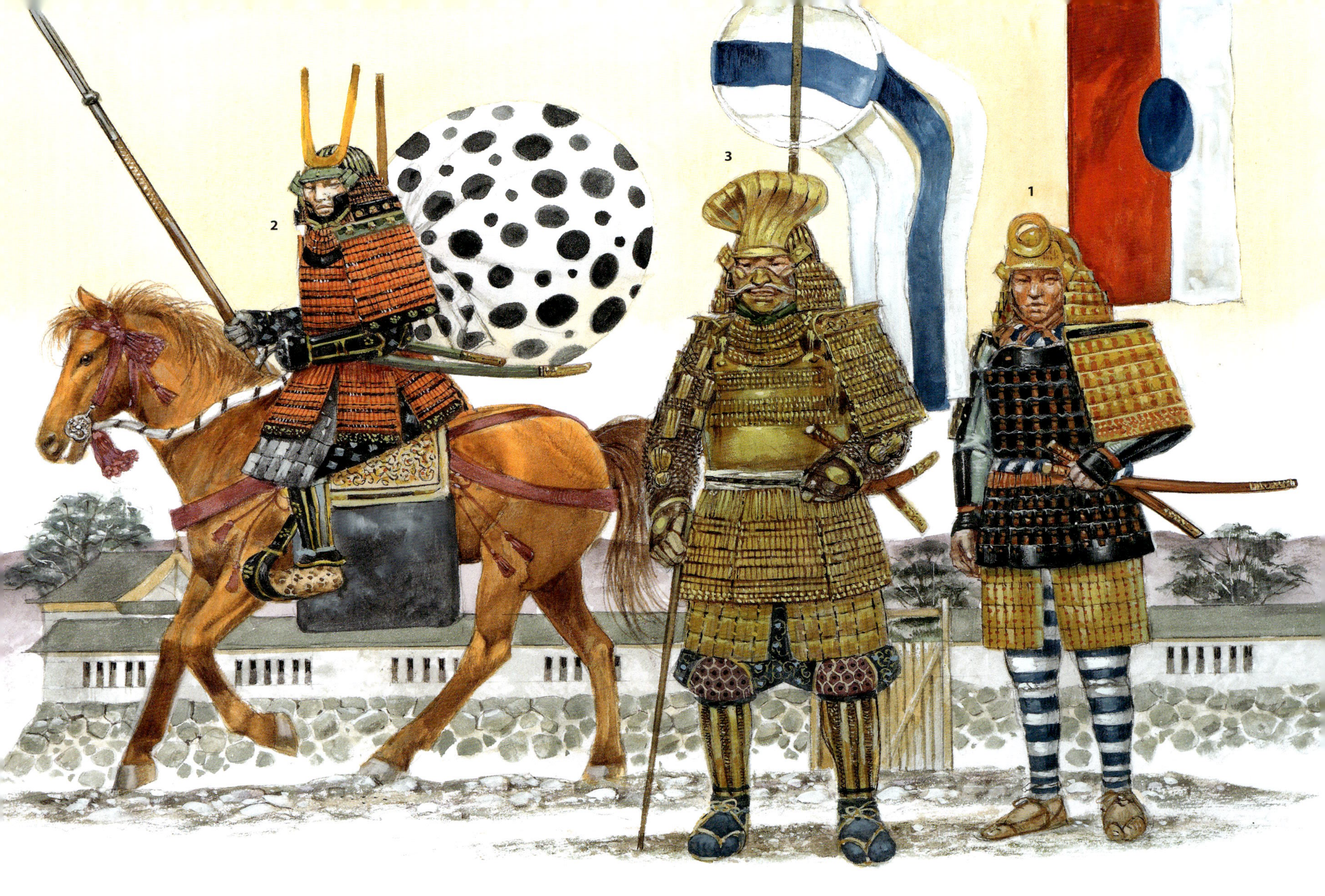
2
3
1

Dstinguished by a red *horo*, and going into action on foot carrying a long iron club, the figure at right is Mogami Yoshiaki, the victor at the battle of Hasedo in 1600.

ditches to be deepened and walls to be strengthened. Although only 300-strong his garrison were determined fighters, and morale was helped during the attack when a ninja infiltrated the Naoe camp and brought back a battle flag, which was then flown in mocking triumph from the main gate. Naoe Kanetsugu eventually triumphed by sheer weight of numbers, and a short march eastwards the following day placed his army in a position from which they could threaten the castle of Hasedo, the last Mogami outpost before Yamagata.

At first Kanetsugu's men set up their *maku* to the west, but there was no immediate attack; instead Kanetsugu moved his base to the mountain of Sugezawa north of the castle, and settled down for a siege. Hasedo Castle was certainly larger than that at Hataya, but his lack of urgency also suggests

Three of Mogami Yoshiaki's hatamoto are shown here at right on the painted scroll of the battle of Hasedo. One has a *gohei sashimono* (see Plate D) and carries a long club; the one at the rear has a more conventional flag *sashimono* and wields a *naginata*.

58

that Kanetsugu was unaware that the Mogami and Date forces had been shadowing his moves, and were almost ready to close in. Whatever his motivation, Naoe Kanetsugu commenced a siege of Hasedo that was to last 15 days. His decision to besiege Hasedo rather than storm it showed that he appreciated the strength of the castle, a conclusion supported by the fact that on arrival he had sent a message to Uesugi Kagekatsu requesting reinforcements.

Hasedo was commanded by Mogami Yoshiaki's hatamoto Shimura Takaharu, who was determined to follow the fine example of loyalty shown at Hataya. Over the following two weeks he did just that, buying time for the arrival of Date and Mogami as he waged a war of attrition against the besiegers. The casualties already suffered by the main Kanetsugu army at Hataya had been considerable, and the second division had also suffered greatly at Kaminoyama and had lost their commander Hommura Chikamori. Meanwhile the joint forces of Mogami and Date were advancing to raise the siege of Hasedo. Date Masamune had delegated the command of his army to his uncle Date Masakage (1549–1607), and the two commands joined forces to the east of Hasedo. On learning of their approach Naoe Kanetsugu ordered an all-out attack on the castle. His vanguard under Kasuga Mototada fought bravely but were stopped at the castle's outer defences by fierce arquebus fire. Kanetsugu then ordered a tactical withdrawal, but as this was happening a sortie was made from the castle that caught the attackers in the rear. Naoe Kanetsugu then decided to abandon the siege of Hasedo and attack the main prize of Yamagata instead. To cover his rear he left a small holding force outside Hasedo; the fighting continued, and another of Kanetsugu's commanders, Kamiizumi Yasutsuna, was killed.

For all his skill and bravery Naoe Kanetsugu was in a very difficult position, but in the event the issue was not going to be resolved by any battle in Tōhoku. While Kanetsugu was on his fighting retreat northwards a courier guardsman arrived from his daimyo Uesugi Kagekatsu with serious news. The pro-Hideyori coalition under Ishida Mitsunari to which they belonged had been defeated in western Japan at the battle of Sekigahara. The seriousness of this defeat may not have been appreciated immediately, but the courier brought orders for Naoe Kanetsugu to retreat to Yonezawa and safety. Date and Mogami also received word of Sekigahara at about the same time, and redoubled their efforts to catch Kanetsugu before he could withdraw. His rearguard was therefore harassed as he moved south, eventually arriving at Uesugi Kagekatsu's castle of Aizu-Wakamatsu.

Naoe Kanetsugu was the great defeated hero of the Uesugi side at the battle of Hasedo in 1600. Sent there by his master Uesugi Kagekatsu, he conducted a 15-day siege before learning that the battle of Sekigahara had nullified any possible result.

Throughout the whole of the Tōhoku Sekigahara campaign Uesugi Kagekatsu, the great northern daimyo on whose behalf the campaign had been waged, had never left the safety of his own fortress. All the fighting had been done by his hatamoto, but if Kagekatsu thought that this would soften his fate he was much mistaken. Tokugawa Ieyasu deprived him of Aizu-Wakamatsu Castle and greatly reduced his fief; its main castle became Yonezawa, where the brave hatamoto Naoe Kanetsugu had been based. Naoe Kanestugu continued to serve Uesugi Kagekatsu after the latter pledged allegiance to Ieyasu, and was with him during the Winter Campaign of Osaka, where several daimyo like Kagekatsu were required to prove in battle the worth of their allegiance. Kanetsugu eventually died in 1620 at the age of 60.

THE SATAKE HATAMOTO AT OSAKA, 1614
The battle of Imafuku

The Satake family under Satake Yoshinobu were the ultimate beneficiaries of the wars fought in the Akita area, but their transfer away from Hitachi to this remote northern territory had never been a reward, rather a thinly-veiled punishment for their tardy decision to submit to the Tokugawa. The incident at Rokugo had shown how unwelcome they were to the local inhabitants, but Satake Yoshinobu had to prove to the Tokugawa not only that he could manage his new territory but that he could be as loyal as any *fudai* daimyo. Just as for Uesugi Kagekatsu, the opportunity to do this came with the Winter Campaign of Osaka in 1614. We noted above that the Satake army took part in the battle of Imafuku that helped to secure the communications routes around Osaka Castle. The Satake *karō* Shibue Naizen Masateru was killed there, but he was only one of a number of Satake hatamoto who distinguished themselves in that battle, thus finally cementing their master's position with the Tokugawa shogun.

Two veteran hatamoto of the Satake who fought at Imafuku were Nakamura Mitsumasa and Okabe Gorō'emon, and they reminisced before the battle about the happy times they had spent together when they were comrades in Hitachi. They were now both more than 60 years old, and decided that as it had been their fate to have been born in the same year, so they should welcome their coming destiny even if it meant that they were also to die in the same year. Intoning the Noh chant '*Shigemori*', which tells of the death of a young warrior during the Gempei Wars, they drank a farewell cup of *sake* together; both were to fall in combat the following day.

While in his headquarters position at Imafuku, their daimyo Satake Yoshinobu was

Satake Yoshinobu was one of many daimyo to be seriously affected by the Tokugawa policy of re-allocation of fiefs in 1603. This drawing in Kubota Castle in Akita shows Yoshinobu at the time of his transfer to the inhospitable north-west; the actual armour is preserved in the Satake Memorial Museum. The first problem that Yoshinobu faced in Akita was a revolt by the surviving hatamoto of the exiled Onodera family, who besieged him in his castle of Rokugo.

visited by Furuta Oribe, the noted tea-master. We are not told whether or not he performed the tea ceremony for Yoshinobu prior to his going into battle – which was not unknown in samurai warfare – but it is recorded that Oribe was so dedicated to his art that he began examining the bamboo palisade fence to see if any of the sections was suitable for making a carved teaspoon. While he was doing so a stray bullet hit him in the head; quite unperturbed, he removed a purple tea napkin from his armour and calmly wiped the blood away.

A courier guardsman then arrived from Tokugawa Hidetada, who ordered the Satake army into battle immediately. Although their action was ultimately successful, the Satake were at one stage driven back by a suicidal charge from the Osaka side. One hatamoto of the Satake who was caught up in this was the 24-year-old Tomura Yoshikuni; his fellow hatamoto Shirato Yoshi'emon had just been killed cutting his way into the advancing enemy lines, so Yoshikuni climbed up onto the embankment along with his flag-bearer to follow this fine example of samurai heroism. There he was met by a hail of enemy missiles; two arrows pierced his left arm and several arquebus bullets hit him in the side. As he fell in unbearable pain his retainer Nakayama Shichi'emon jumped down to help him.

Yoshikuni was stunned by his fall, but rose to his feet very unsteadily and tried to make his way again towards the enemy, who momentarily drew back at the spectacle of this bloody apparition. Shichi'emon could see that his master was lapsing into unconsciousness, and as he fell again Shichi'emon took Yoshikuni by the shoulders and tried to drag him back towards the Satake lines. But Yoshikuni was a heavily built man, and still kept a tight hold of his spear, an additional hindrance; though Shichi'emon politely requested him to let go of the weapon he would not abandon it. With a supreme effort the slightly built Shichi'emon dragged him back as far as the edge of some marshy ground; this proved impossible to cross, but just then a samurai appeared on a grey horse, lifted Yoshikuni onto it and took him across the swamp to safety. When Shichi'emon made his way back to the Satake headquarters with Yoshikuni he recounted how the anonymous samurai had helped them, but the mysterious man was never identified, and a legend grew within the Tomura family that he had been a personification of the Buddha.

Uesugi Kagekatsu was defeated by proxy during the Tōhoku Sekigahara campaign and had his revenues drastically reduced by the Tokugawa. Like the Satake clan, he rehabilitated himself at the battle of Imafuku outside Osaka in 1614.

This magnificent lacquered wooden statue is of Tomura Yoshikuni, one of the heroes of the Satake family hatamoto who fought at the battle of Imafuku during the Winter Campaign of Osaka, 1614. The statue stands in his memorial chapel in the family temple beside Yokote Castle.

The following year Tomura Yoshikuni was summoned to Nijo Castle in Kyoto and received from the shogun, Tokugawa Hidetada, an official letter of commendation and a fine sword. Umezu Noritada, the 'Yellow Devil of the Satake clan' also received a letter and a sword for his conduct at Imafuku, while three other Satake hatamoto were also commended and given rewards of gold coins and *jinbaori* (surcoats). Of only 12 letters of commendation granted for conduct at Imafuku, five went to hatamoto from the Satake family; the clan's rehabilitation was complete.

* * *

There is an interesting postscript to the story of Tomura Yoshikuni, because his grandson became the first castellan of Yokote Castle after it had been rebuilt. The headquarters of the Satake clan were now located to the north of Yokote at Kubota Castle (today in the middle of modern Akita city), but the Tomura family were to retain responsibility for Yokote for over two centuries in recognition of the service of their illustrious ancestor. As late as 1868 Yokote once more came under attack, during the Boshin War that was fought between the new imperial government and supporters of the ousted Tokugawa shogun.

Tomura Daigaku, aged 19, was then the keeper of Yokote Castle; enemy forces were advancing deep into the territory from the south just as the Mogami had done centuries earlier, and several castles had been either abandoned or burned, but Tomura Daigaku was made of sterner stuff. Imbued with the spirit of his ancestor Tomura Yoshikuni, he prepared to defend Yokote with a small garrison of only 280 men, and took a considerable personal part in the battle. After two hours of fierce hand-to-hand fighting, during which Tomura Daigaku killed two men, he escaped with the survivors of the garrison. He lived to a ripe old age, becoming the mayor of Yokote after peace had descended upon newly modernized Japan. In a wood below the castle lies the Tomura family's ancestral Buddhist temple, and in a small chapel there stands a lacquered wooden statue of the hatamoto Tomura Yoshikuni, whose determined aspect must have inspired young Daigaku; with ancestors like that, you don't surrender….

BIBLIOGRAPHY & FURTHER READING

My sources for the stories of the hatamoto of the Onodera and the Satake families are taken largely from '*Ou Eikei Gunki*', which forms volumes 3 and 4 of the series '*Sengoku Shiryō Sōshō*', and has recently been republished in an abridged single-volume edition under the name of the editor Imamura Yoshitaka (Tokyo, 2005). A straightforward account of the Onodera-Mogami battles is '*Kosenjō – Akita no kassen shi*', compiled by a historical group in Akita and published there in 1981. More detailed accounts of the Onodera, including the fall of Nishimonai Castle, are taken from '*Onodera uji no genryū to kōbō shi*' by Onodera Takeshi (Tokyo, 1988). The exploits of the Satake at Osaka appear in '*Ogawa yūkyū no Satake ke*' by Doi Teruo (Tokyo, 2002). Two recent works by Sasama Yoshihiko, '*Nihon Kassen Zuten*' (1997) and '*Nihon Senjin Sahō Jiten*' (2000) are each valuable for matters of army organization, and I have used these books in particular for the details about the structure and appearance of the Tokugawa guards units.

Kimura Tsudarō, a late Edo Period hatamoto of Nihonmatsu, was killed at the age of 22 during the defence of Nihonmatsu Castle in the Boshin War of 1868. He is shown in the scroll in the Nihonmatsu Museum wearing traditional samurai costume and carrying an arquebus.

INDEX

References to illustrations are shown in **bold**.
Plates are shown with page locators in brackets.

Aizu-Wakamatsu Castle 55, 59, 60
Akechi Mitsuhide 30, 33–4
Anegawa, battle of 8, 10–11, **10**, **11**, 42, 47, 50, **G(51)**
armour 6, 7, 8, **A(9)**, 19, 28, 30, **D(31)**, 35, 36, **E(37)**, 38, 39, 44, 49, 50, 56, **H(57)**, 60, 61
arquebuses/arquebusiers 18, 19, 26, 30, 38, 42, 44, 47, 49, 52, 59, 61, 63
Asai Nagamasa 30, 47
Asai Shimpachi 8, **A(9)**
Asakura army 10–11, **10**, 28, 42
Asakura Kagetake 10–11, **10**
ashigaru footsoldiers (*dōshin*) 21, 22, 38, **38**
Azuchi Castle 29, 32, 33

banners, vertical (*nobori*) 5, 8, 8, 19, 36, **E(37)**, 40, 41, **41**, 53, 54
Body Guard (*Shōin Ban*) 34, 56, **H(57)**
bow-bearers/bow units 19, 42
bows and arrows 5, 15, 18, 19, 26, 30, 38, 42, 52, 61

chief retainer (*karō*) 13, 14, 15, 16, 27, 47, 49, 60
Chōkōji Castle, siege of 13
Colour Guards 10, 40–1
commissioners (*bugyō*) 18–19, 36, **E(37)**, 47
Courier Guards 25, 35–6, **35**, 36, **E(37)**, 40, 44, **F(45)**, 59, 61

Date Masamune **19**, 48, 50, 55, 59

Endō Naotsugu **11**
Escort Guards 38–9, 38, 56, **H(57)**

farmer-samurai, actions of 47, 48, 50, 53
field HQs 7, 10, 16, **B(17)**, 19, 42, 44
flag-bearers/flag squads 36, **E(37)**, 40, 61
flags (*hata*) 4, 8, 8, 10, **11**, 26, 36, **E(37)**, 42, 58
  decoration 35, **36**, 41, 42, 44, **F(45)**, 56
  personal devices 6, 8, 14, 40, 41, 50
  signalling devices 19, 35, 40, 41, **41**, 42
Foot Guards 38–43, **38**, 44, **F(45)**, 56, **H(57)**
footsoldiers (*ashigaru*) 16, **B(17)**, 18, 21, 26, 38, 41–3, 44, **F(45)**, 47
funerary tablet (*ihai*) 30, **D(31)**

generals (*taishō*) 18, 36, **E(37)**, 41
Great Guard (*Oban/Ogoban*) 21, 34

haori (sleeveless jacket) 44, **48**
Hasedo, battle of **56**, 58, 59
Hasedo Castle, siege of 58–9
hatamoto (daimyo's staff/household troops)
  definition of 4–5, 6, 7, 20
  delegation of command duties to 16, 18, 19, 34, 47, 55, 56, 58, 59, 60
  peacetime roles 20–2, **21**, 24–5, 24, 53
  protection by 4, 5, 6–7, 7, 8, 10–11, 10, **11**, 12, 12, 13, 13, 15, 18, 20–1, **20**, 21, 22, 24, 25, 25, 30, 33–4, 43, 46, 47, 47, 49, 50, 53, 58, 59, 60, 61, 62, 63
Hataya Castle, fall of 56, 58, 59
heads (enemy) **11**, 15, **15**, 16, 18, 20, **26**, 29, 30, 42, 46, 49, 50, **G(51)**, 55
'heavenly kings' (Shitennō) 4, 5, 5, 6, 10
helmet-bearers 16, **B(17)**, 30, **D(31)**, 42
helmets (*kabuto*) 8, **A(9)**, 16, **B(17)**, 30, **D(31)**, 38, 39, 49, 50, 56, **H(57)**
Hōjō army/family 25, 26, **26**, 30, **D(31)**, 44, **F(45)**, 48, 50, **G(51)**
Hojo Ujiyasu 25, **26**
Honda Tadakatsu 14, 36, **E(37)**
Honnōji temple, attack on 30, 33
Honourable New Guard (Goshoinban) 34, 35
horo (cloaks) 8, **A(9)**, 22, **C(23)**, **29**, 32, 34, 36, 44, **F(45)**, 50, **G(51)**, 56, **H(57)**, 58

Horo Horse Guards 8, **A(9)**, **27**, 29–30, **29**, 32–3, 34
  Black Horo 8, **A(9)**, 32
  Great Horo/War Fan 22, **C(23)**, 34
  Red Horo 8, **A(9)**, 22, **C(23)**, 32, 34
  Yellow Horo 22, **C(23)**, 34

Ikkō-ikki armies 13–14, 15, 40
Imafuku, battle of **14**, 16, 60–1, **61**, 62
Imagawa Yoshimoto 13, 20, 29
Imayama, battle of 43, 44
Inner Guard (*Koshōban*) 34
inner lords (*fudai daimyo*) 20, 21, 54, 60
inspectors (*metsuke/yokome*) **15**, 19–20

Kaminoyama Castle, attack on 56, 59
Katakura Kagetsuna **19**
Katō Kiyomasa 39, **40**
Kawajiri Hidetaka 8, **A(9)**
Kawanakajima, battle of 35, 40–1, 43–4, 43, 48
Kimura Tsudarō 63
Kinoshita Genzan 30, **D(31)**
Kiyosu Castle 27
Kojima Yatarō **46**
Korea, invasion of 16, **B(17)**, 48, 49
Kunohe Castle, rebellion at 48
Kuroda Nagasama 16, **B(17)**
Kuruma Tamba-no-kami 30, **D(31)**

Maeda Toshiie 8, **A(9)**, **27**, 29, 29
Makara Jurōzaemon Naotaka 10–11, **10**
maku (curtains) 6, 7, 7, 8, 10, 16, **B(17)**, 18, **25**, 29, 35, 36, **E(37)**, 52, 53, 58
  attacks on 11, 43–4, 46, 47, 48, 50
Matsu Hidenobu 50, **G(51)**
Matsumae Castle 24
Matsuoko Kurojiro 8, **A(9)**
Miki Castle, attack on 34
Minamoto Yoshitsune 4, 5, 6, 8, 10, 52
Mitsukuriyama Castle, attack on 8, **A(9)**, 32
Miyajima, battle of 18
Mogami army/family 47, 48–9, 50, 52–3, 54, 56, 58–9, 62
Mogami Yoshiaki 48–9, 52–3, **52**, 54, 55, 56, 58–9, 58
Mōri Motonari **18**
Mukai Masatsuna 44, **F(45)**
Mukai Shogen Tadakatsu 44, **F(45)**

Nagahama Castle, capture of 34
Nagakute, battle of **36**, 41
Nagashino, battle of **11**, 20
Naoe Kanetsugu 55, 56, 58, 59, **59**, 60
nembutsu funerary ritual 42, 43
New Guard (*Shinban*) 56, **H(57)**
Nihonmatsu Castle, defence of 63
Nishimonai Castle, fall of 47, 53–4, 55, 63
Nishi-no-maru 34, 35, 39, 56, **H(57)**

Oba Nobunaga 8, **A(9)**, 10, **11**, 12, 13, 13, 15, 22, **C(23)**, 28, 29, 30, 30, 32, 33, 34, 40, 57
Oda Nobutada 29, 33
Odawara, battle of 44, **F(45)**, 48, 50, **G(51)**
Okabe Gonnoday **26**, 50, **G(51)**
Okehazama, battle of 13, 20, 29, **29**, 33, 43
Okubo Shichiro'emon Tadayo 50, **G(51)**
Omori Castle, action against 47, 49, 50, 52, 53
Ono Castle, attack on 48–9
Onodera army/family 18, 47, 48–50, 52, 52, 53–4, 53, 55, 55, 60, 63
Onodera Shigemichi 47, 53, 54, 55
Onodera Yasumichi 47, 50, 53
Onodera Yoshimichi 47, 49, 53, 54, 63
Osaka, battles of **15**, 21, 25, 36, 60, **61**, 62, 63
Osaka Castle, siege of 14, 16, 44, **F(45)**, 60
Otani army 50, 52
Otani Yoshitsugu 50, 52, 53
Otomo Chikasada 44, 46
outer lords (*tozama*) 21, 54

pages and squires (*koshō*) 8, **A(9)**, 21, **27**, 29, **29**, 30, 33, 34, 39–40, **39**, 44
pole-arms (*naginata*) 42, 49, 53, 58
priests (*jishū*), as 'army chaplains' 42–3
rakes (*ō-kumade*), use of 50, **G(51)**
ritual suicide (*seppuku*) 6, 49, 52, 55
Rokugo Castle, siege of 55, 60, **60**
rōnin (masterless *samurai*) 21, 24, 25, 54

Saga Castle, siege of 44
Sakai Masanao 28, 47
Sakai Narishige 47
Sakai Tadasugu **11**
Sakenobe Norikatsu 53–4
sashimono (back-flags) **11**, 22, **C(23)**, 25, 26, 30, **D(31)**, 34, 35, 36, **E(37)**, 39, 44, **F(45)**, 46, 50, **G(51)**, 54, 56, **H(57)**
Sassa Narimasa **27**
Satake army/family **14**, 16, 60, **61**, 62, 63
Satake Yoshinobu 16, 54, 55, 60–1, **60**, 63
secretaries (*yūhitsu*) **15**, 42
Sekigahara, battle of 7, 20, 24, 36, **E(37)**, 40, 50, **G(51)**, 52, 53, 53, 54, 55, 59, 59
Shibata Katsuie 13, 15
Shibue Naizen Masateru 16, 60
Shima Sakon 54
Shimazu Yoshihori 33
Shimabara, battle of 21
Shiroishi Castle **19**
spear-carriers/spear squads 19, 42, 49
spears **11**, 15, 18, 19, 26, 29, 38, 42, 44, 49, 50, 61
standard-bearers 8, 10, 36, **E(37)**, 40, 41, 44, **F(45)**, 54
standards 4, 16, **B(17)**, 34, 36, **E(37)**, 44, **F(45)**
streamers (*fukinuki*) 6, 8, 35, **54**, 56, **H(57)**
Sue Harakuta, death of 18
swords 6, 10, **10**, 22, 30, 39, 44, 62

Takeda army/family 36, 40, 43, 44, **F(45)**
Takeda Katsuyori 33, 44, **F(45)**
Takeda Shingen **18**, **20**, 35, 41, 42, 43–4, 48
Toda Castle **49**
Tōdō Takatora 16, **B(17)**
Tōhoku Sekigahara Campaign 30, **D(31)**, 47–9, 50, 52, 55–6, 58–60, 61
Tokugawa army/family 14, 16, 20, 21–2, 24, 25, 30, **D(31)**, 34, 36, 44, **F(45)**, 50, **G(51)**, 61, 63
Tokugawa Hidetada 21, 61, 62
Tokugawa Iemitsu 35, 38, 56, **H(57)**
Tokugawa Ieyasu 5, 7, 8, 10, **10**, **11**, 12–13, 14–15, 16, 20, 24, 25, 33, 34, 36, **E(37)**, 44, **F(45)**, 47, 50, **G(51)**, 52, 53, 54–5, 60, 60
Tomura Yoshikuni 61, 62, **62**, 63
Toyotomi Hidetsugu 12, 55
Toyotomi Hideyori 24–5, 52, 53, 55, 59
Toyotomi Hideyoshi 12, 16, **B(17)**, 22, **C(23)**, 25, 27, 33, 34, 39, 40, 48, 49–50, 52, **52**, 53, 55, 57
Tsunashima Shōheimon 56

Uesugi army 41, 43, **43**, 44
Uesugi Kagekatsu 36, 55–6, 58, 59, **59**, 60, 61
Uesugi Kenshin 43, **43**, 44, **46**, 48
Umezu Noritada **14**, 16, **19**, 62

war fans 22, **C(23)**, 34, 38, 40, 44, 56
Watanabe Hanzō Moritsuna 14, 15

Yabe Toranosuke 30, **D(31)**
Yamagata Castle, siege of 48, **52**, 56, 58, 59
Yamanaka Shikanosuke **49**
Yamazaki, battle of 22, **C(23)**
Yokote Castle 47, 49, 53, 55, 62–3, **62**
Yonezawa Castle 56, 59, 60
yoriki 21, 22, 38, 47
Yuki Harutomo/Masakatsu 26–7
Yuki Horse Guards 28–9
Yuzawa Castle, fall of 49, 50